"This book ha˜ ˜˜˜˜˜˜ ˜˜˜˜˜˜˜ number of financial products for the accumulation and decumulation stages of one's life, and explained the products in an engaging and clear manner, without overlaying too much technical information. I feel that the coverage of the book is excellent for most people who are not specialists in the investment world, and even has much information for those of us who specialize in investments and insurance. Although I have been teaching in these areas for over 25 years and have worked on Wall Street, I learned a lot and plan to use this book as a helpful guide to financial planning for my own retirement."

—*Dave Babbel, professor of insurance and finance,*
The Wharton School of Business

"*Fiscal Fitness* breaks down barriers between fitness and finances—explaining why both are so important to enjoying a full life. In *Fiscal Fitness*, Jack LaLanne and Matthew J. Rettick provide readers with sound advice and a 'game plan' for achieving health and wealth for a lifetime."

—*Jeff Fisher, NFL head coach, Tennessee Titans*

"Whether fiscal, physical, or getting ready for a ballgame, it's all in the preparation. LaLanne was a childhood hero of mine. Matthew Rettick has become an adult hero of mine. Matthew and Jack show you how to push to stay in shape physically and financially so that you can pull out a 'fun' retirement. Now, get back to work!!"

—*Mike Veeck, author of* Fun is Good, *co-owner of*
five minor-league baseball teams, including the
Charleston RiverDogs

"The wisdom of Jack LaLanne has inspired generations of Americans to get healthy. In this book, LaLanne and Matthew Rettick make us healthy, wealthy, and wise. Ageless and priceless reading. I recommend it!"

—*Jordan Rubin, author of* New York Times
best-seller The Maker's Diet, *and*
founder and CEO of The Garden of Life

"Considered the Godfather of Fitness, Jack LaLanne KNOWS fitness. He has been impacting lives for over 70 years, which is why the President's Council on Physical Fitness and Sports honored him with a Lifetime Achievement Award. He is a successful pioneer in the health and fitness industry."

—*Melissa Johnson, executive director, President's Council on Physical Fitness and Sports*

"It is brilliant to bring the areas of financial and physical fitness together! As someone who has officially entered my 50s, these are the two areas of greatest concern and challenge for me. As my financial advisor, Matthew Rettick has helped position me for future financial security. For those who want to live life to the fullest, this book is a must-read!!"

—*Nancy Alcorn, founder of Mercy Ministries*

"*Fiscal Fitness* is full of expert advice. Jack LaLanne and Matthew J. Rettick provide readers with a clear roadmap to achieving health and wealth today, tomorrow, and years ahead."

—*Ken Dychtwald, PhD, author of* The Power Years: A User's Guide to the Rest of Your Life

"This is the rare book that not only shows you how to live longer and healthier, but also have the financial security to really enjoy those extra years."

—*Ed Slott, author of* Your Complete Retirement Planning Road Map

"*Fiscal Fitness* will be the blueprint for successful, vibrant aging! Jack LaLanne and Matthew Rettick have blended their talents and energy to create relevant solutions for physical and financial longevity."

—*Deborah Redder, creator of the SilverSneakers Group Exercise Program, and Healthways director-instructor, development and activity programming*

"*Fiscal Fitness* offers clear and practical advice that's better than gold! Do what these two legends suggest, and you too will see your financial and physical health improve beyond measure! It's a must-read!"

—*Alan W. Altmann, international speaker and author*

"I have always believed that we are four-part creatures: spirit, mind, body, and wallet. Get the latter two in shape and you'll be amazed at what happens to your spirit and mind. If you don't believe it, let the latter two go and see how well you do. Matt Rettick and Jack LaLanne are two people who can help you get a complete Fiscal check-up and put together a training program that will not only help you live long, but to live long *and* well!"

—*Mitch Anthony, author of* The New RetireMentality

"If you neglect your physical or financial fitness, you will jeopardize your retirement. It's that simple. Matt Rettick and Jack LaLanne offer solid advice for both the body and the bank account. This book is rich with information on how you can take immediate action and get control of the two most important elements to a long, healthy retirement—your financial and physical health."

—*Dan Wiesner, CEO, Wiesner Publishing, Inc.*

"Whether you have already hit the Big Five-Oh or live in that neighborhood, everyone needs to be planning now for the *second*—and perhaps the best—*50 years of life*. I Can think of no better coaches for a vibrant Second 50 than Jack LaLanne and Matthew Rettick."

—*Daniel Perry, executive director,*
Alliance for Aging Research

"Health and money may be the two most frightening issues facing Americans today...but Jack LaLanne and Matthew Rettick have a plan that works! *Fiscal Fitness* combines the wit, passion, and accumulated wisdom of these two great masters into a fun and powerful program for success."

—*Frank Maselli, CIMC, president,*
The Frank Maselli Company, Inc.
Advanced Training for Financial Professionals

"Living Longer, more prosperous lives is a goal aspired to by most Americans, and talked about by many politicians. Now, Matthew Rettick and Jack LaLanne show you how to take control of your physical and financial futures. If you are ready to make positive changes for your future, you must read *Fiscal Fitness*."

—Kevin R. Wingert, president,
American Investment Life Insurance Company

"In these pages, Jack LaLanne and Matthew J. Rettick guide you through your two major obstacles, the critical physical and financial hurdles, all the way to your goals. Follow their plans and you will enjoy tremendous results."

—Charles "Tremendous" Jones, author of
Life is Tremendous

"My late husband, Loren Dunton, created financial planning, and founded the multi-trillion-dollar financial planning industry. Loren would consider *Fiscal Fitness* to be of historical importance in the evolution of personal financial planning."

—Marta Dunton (the "first lady" of financial
planning), widow of the founder of financial planning

"*Fiscal Fitness* is the most beneficial book ever for achieving physical and financial success, starting at any age. Jack LaLanne and Matthew J. Rettick have created a unique volume that is certain to become a best-seller among financial and self-help titles."

—Forrest Wallace Cato, RFMA, RFC, editor of
Fiduciary Legal Report *and* Success Plan,
former editor of Financial Planning *and* Trust & Estates
magazines, and author of
Terrible Truth About Financial Planning

Fiscal

Fitness

8 Steps to Wealth & Health From America's Leaders of Fitness and Finance

Jack LaLanne
Matthew J. Rettick

CAREER
PRESS

Franklin Lakes, NJ

FISCAL FITNESS
EDITED BY KARA REYNOLDS
TYPESET BY MICHAEL FITZGIBBON
Cover design by Rob Johnson/Johnson Design
Printed in the U.S.A. by Book-mart Press

To order this title, please call toll-free 1-800-CAREER-1 (NJ and Canada: 201-848-0310) to order using VISA or MasterCard, or for further information on books from Career Press.

P CAREER
PRESS

The Career Press, Inc., 3 Tice Road, PO Box 687,
Franklin Lakes, NJ 07417
www.careerpress.com

Library of Congress Cataloging-in-Publication Data
LaLanne, Jack, 1914–
    Fiscal fitness : 8 steps to wealth and health from America's leaders of fitness and finance / by Jack LaLanne and Matthew J. Rettick.
        p. cm.
    Includes index.
    ISBN 978-1-56414-988-6
    1. Finance, Personal. 2. Physical fitness. I. Rettick, Matthew J. II. Title.

HG179.L253 2008
332.024—dc22
                                                                2007046872

Dedication

To the love of my life, the wind beneath my wings: Linda Kay. Her mercy, grace, and support of me are ever-present. She is not only my wonderful wife, but my soul mate. To my children: Greg, Candy, Jeremy, Brandon, and our 13 grandchildren—you are my reason for living.

To my mother, Ruth. Your confidence and belief in me has helped me overcome many obstacles in life.

—Matthew J. Rettick

To my family: Elaine, Yvonne, and her husband, Mark; Jon Allen and his wife, Lora; and my son, Dan; and all the people who have believed and supported me throughout the years.

—Jack LaLanne

"My child, don't lose sight of good planning and insight. Hang on to them, for they fill you with life and bring you honor and respect. They keep you safe on your way and keep your feet from stumbling."

Proverbs 3:21–23

Acknowledgments

This book had its genesis in 1980, after my maternal grandmother—Grandma Wick—was diagnosed with Alzheimer's disease. Watching her slowly drift away without the proper medical insurance to afford the right kind of care left a lasting impression on me. Then, in 1986, I again watched as nursing-home costs ate away at the life savings of my paternal grandparents, Grandpa and Grandma Rettick.

The severity of what I witnessed because my grandparents hadn't planned properly for their future—what was supposed to be their golden years—planted in me the seeds of compassion and commitment to help others avoid the same costly consequences. This book, I hope, will spur you, too, to look into your own future and prepare now for *fiscal and financial fitness* in your golden years.

I am most indebted to my good friend and coauthor, Jack LaLanne, and his lovely wife, Elaine. From a tiny seed, a mighty oak tree forms and develops. Jack is not only a mighty example of and force for physical fitness, but he and Elaine are also two of the most down-to-earth, caring, loving celebrities one could ever meet. It has been a pleasure to work with Jack, who has been my company's national celebrity spokesperson these past three years, and to collaborate on the most important message Americans need to hear and heed.

Special thanks also go to the following:

- Susan J. Marks, a journalist and writer who was instrumental in formulating the concepts of two different worlds into one concise, easy-to-follow, step-by-step guide.

- Phyllis Shelton of LTC Consultants®, the number-one advocate in this nation for long-term-care insurance.
- Dean Zayed of Brookstone Capital Management, a master communicator for financial advisors and consumers on the importance of diversifying one's retirement dollars into effective money-management platforms and stable low-risk accounts.
- Andy Smith, an invaluable resource on accurate and current information on veterans' benefits.
- Cynthia Zigmund, our fabulous book agent, and a great supporter of this book's message and mission. The early success of this project was a direct result of her expertise and negotiating skills.
- TC, my friend and colleague, whom I credit with the original concept of this book.
- Members of my staff were great contributors as well: Kevin Vozar, Joe Stamps, Pete Winer, Tony Dolle, and Mary Grace Ammons.

To all of these fine people and many more, I say thank you.

Matthew J. Nettis

Special thanks to my wife, Elaine, my son, Dan, and my good friend, Gale Rudolph, PhD, for assisting me in the preparation of this book. Because my computer skills are limited, their help was invaluable in transcribing my words and researching my archives, as well as those online, to provide our readers with the latest statistics and information about maintaining a healthy lifestyle.

Jack La Lanne

CONTENTS

Foreword

By Art Linkletter

Nobody dies only of old age, but everyone *hastens* their departure if they live life *carelessly*. If you don't care about good health habits and exercise, or if you let financial problems worry you to death, then you only have yourself to blame.

As chairman of the board at the UCLA Center on Aging, I have had many years of studying the miracle of long life. I say miracle because in my lifetime, the average age has gone from 47 to 77, and right now the fastest-growing population is 85 years and up. Today's 60 is yesterday's 40. And books like this one are in step with the times and the needs.

It's never too late to start exercising, and if you really work at it, you can see some astonishing results. For proof, look no further than the hoards of athletes in their 60s, 70s, 80s, and 90s competing in track and field, swimming, and other athletic events in the Senior Olympics. On a personal note, at the age of 95, I swim almost every day, lift weights, and do 15 to 30 minutes daily on the stationary bike. I surfed in Hawaii every year and just recently gave up skiing the various "black diamond" trails—my wife gave away my ski clothes while I was on a lecture tour; she said she was worried about me with all the snowboarders, and wanted to be a wife, not a nurse.

Few people are more qualified to talk about exercise on an aging body than Jack LaLanne, who still works out every morning and constantly holds court on the transformative power of movement. He recently told me in an interview:

> *Old age, you have to work at it. Dying is easy. Any stupid person can die. The average American works at dying. Exercise is king. Nutrition is queen. Put them together, you have a kingdom. The only way you can hurt the human body is inactivity, sitting on your big fat butt, thinking about the good old days. The good old days are right this moment. Too many old people say, my mother or father was fat, so they inherited it. The only think you inherit is the color of your hair or eyes; the rest is you. There's no quick fix; you've got to work at it with the 640 muscles in your body that need strength work, flexibility work, and cardiovascular work.*

In my work at UCLA, I've discovered that the release of endorphins produced in the brain through physical activity results in the positive enhancement of your mood. You improve your ability to function, promoting a sense of well-being. Physical activity has proven to stimulate growth in new brain cells and help maintain alertness and mental capacity by challenging the mind to focus, coordinate and process new movements. In other words, as Jack says "If you want to live, *move.*"

Being physically fit, however, is only half the equation for enjoying your life for many years to come. You also need to be financially fit! It doesn't make sense to achieve one without the other. You can really only enjoy your life now and in the next 30, 40, or 50 years to come if you have both accounts in great shape—physical and financial fitness!

Financial expert Matthew J. Rettick is *your* financial coach. He has been recognized by industry experts as the "Man with the Plan." With almost 20 years devoted to helping retirees and pre-retirees achieve their financial goals for retirement, Matt's the right man for the job!

Read this book and live abundantly, as I have for 95 years! Jack LaLanne has been my friend and mentor for the last 40 years, so you can believe me when I say, take Jack and Matt's 8 Steps to Health and Wealth, and take charge of your life!

Introduction

Your physical and financial fitness—or lack thereof—affects your entire life, especially your retirement years. Paying attention to both forms of fitness insures you against catastrophic illness and bolsters the chances that you'll enjoy a comfortable, worry-free retirement, and live a long, healthy life.

Ignore your physical fitness—as in, get little exercise and eat poorly—and chances are you won't live as long as possible. Postpone your retirement planning—as, in refuse to pay attention to what you spend and save, and fail to prepare for tomorrow—and your money won't last as long as it could either.

Fiscal Fitness is about recognizing the importance of and learning how to achieve physical and financial fitness no matter your age. It's neither a typical exercise book nor a standard money book. Instead, it's a unique combination of both—and more—that will help you understand the significance of getting fit, and, step-by-step, what it takes to stay healthy money-wise and body-wise, so you truly can enjoy your later years.

Ideally, we all hope to remain healthy physically and financially until we die so that we never need to worry about what to do in case we aren't. Realistically, however, the situation is a bit less than ideal. In fact, America and Americans are in a financial and health crisis, which often culminates in struggle and hardship for retirees and their loved ones. Consider a few facts:

- Thanks to breakthroughs in medicine, Americans live longer today. The average life expectancy for a male is about 74 years, and a female, almost 80 years. That's up from ages 65 and 71 a half-century ago (National Center for Health Statistics, see *www.cdc.gov/nchs/fastats/lifexpec.htm*). The longevity is great news. But it also means that retirement money must last longer. How much longer depends on your health and the ability to access the care you need.

- If you're age 55 today and live to age 90, you'll need to have accumulated $210,000 by age 65 just to pay for insurance to supplement Medicare and out-of-pocket medical expenses in retirement (Employee Benefit Research Institute® Issue Brief No. 254, February 2003, "Retiree Health Benefits: Savings Needed to Fund Health Care in Retirement," *www.ebri.org/pdf/publications/facts/fastfacts/fastfact050807.pdf*.)

- Almost half of workers saving for retirement say they have less than $25,000 (not including the value of their primary residence or any defined benefit plans) set aside for retirement savings. (2007 Retirement Confidence Survey, Employee Benefit Research Institute®, *www.ebri.org/pdf/briefspdf/EBRI_IB_04a-20075.pdf*).

- Often-preventable chronic diseases—specifically heart disease, cancer, and stroke—have been the leading cause of deaths of those ages 65 and up for the past two decades (National Center for Health Statistics, "Mortality Report." Hyattsville, MD, U.S. Department of Health and Human Services, 2002, *www.cdc.gov/nchs/data/ahcd/ agingtrends/06olderpersons.pdf*).

- An estimated 119 million Americans are overweight or obese (Health, United States, 2003; Atlanta, Georgia: Centers for Disease Control and Prevention, National Center on Vital Statistics, 2003, Table 68). As a result, those people can be at higher risk for a variety of ailments and chronic diseases (U.S. Centers for Disease Control and Prevention).

- Long-term care costs are soaring. The 2007 average daily rate for a private room in a nursing home is $213 ($77,745 annually), a $7 or 3.4 percent increase over the 2006 rate of $206 (The MetLife Mature Market Institute).

- Almost seven out of ten, or 69 percent, of seniors (those age 65 and older in 2005) will need long-term care—whether convalescent care, home healthcare, skilled nursing care, or adult day care—at some time during the rest of their lives [Peter Kemper, Harriet Komisar, and Lisa Alexcih, "Long-Term Care over an Uncertain Future: What Can Current Retirees Expect?" *Inquiry* 42, No. 4: 335–350 (2006)].

- One out of three seniors (35 percent) will need nursing-home care (Kemper, Komisar, and Alexcih, "Long-Term Care").

These numbers hit home for all of us. In fact, for many Americans the fear of dying shortly after retirement has been replaced by the fear of outliving one's assets. Almost two in 10 baby boomers, those born post-World War II through 1964, say they won't have enough money in retirement for basic living expenses (Pew Research Center statistics).

Yet, unfortunately, our government offers few, if any, solutions. Despite what many people think, Medicare doesn't pay for long-term care (it picks up only the cost—with co-pays—for a maximum 100 days associated with each hospitalization). As mentioned, such care is not cheap. Today the cost of long-term care can amount to anywhere from a few thousand dollars a month to $10,000 and up. Families become stressed and strapped, and the aging parent or loved one is left with apparently few resources and little or no recourse. He or she may not start out broke, but often is forced into poverty in order to qualify for medical welfare in the form of Medicaid, which will pick up the tab for nursing-home care.

Even some who don't require full-time care often end up in nursing homes because they see no alternatives for getting care and financial relief from the soaring cost of care. But options are available *if* you plan ahead and make the right choices *before it's too late*. (Remember the old adage, "An ounce of prevention is worth of pound of cure"? It still holds true.)

With a few simple moves, we all can increase our chances of living a long, healthy life, and guarantee that if anything unfortunate happens, we and our loved ones will be taken care of financially. Being prepared doesn't take a ton of money, but it does take awareness, conviction, and the right steps today.

Studies by health and medical experts show that a healthier lifestyle, including regular physical activity, a healthy diet, and a smoke-free environment, can reduce the risk of chronic disease. Financial planning and legal experts easily show how a little money spent today can save you a bundle later in terms of your retirement and long-term-care future.

With our help and a little effort, you too can get physically and financially fit, so you can enjoy your life, as well as the lives of those around you, today and throughout your retirement.

Fitness guru Jack LaLanne and longtime retirement-planning expert Matthew J. Rettick are the perfect team to help you get started on this path to fitness.

LaLanne, often called the father of modern fitness, has spent more than seven decades coaching others on what it takes to get healthy, stay healthy, and live a fulfilling life. At age 93, he works out twice a day, is in demand as a motivational speaker nationwide, and, to celebrate his 93rd birthday, he launched a new Internet radio show! (Catch *Jack LaLanne Live*, Monday mornings on VoiceAmerica.com's Health and Wellness Channel.)

But he didn't start out as a specimen of fitness. As a teen he was a *sugarholic* overeater with pimples and boils, and on a path of physical destruction. At 15, ill health forced him to drop out of school for six months. Discouraged, he attended a health lecture and suddenly woke up to the importance of paying attention to health and fitness today as insurance for a sound tomorrow. He joined the local YMCA and bought a copy of *Gray's Anatomy,* reading it cover to cover. He also set up a gym in his backyard and invented, then built, special exercise equipment. Firefighters and police officers who couldn't pass annual physicals came to work out on his equipment.

In the mid-1930s, when he opened the nation's first state-of-the-art health club in Oakland, California, people made fun of him and his ideas of physical fitness. They called him a muscleman, crackpot, and health nut. He advocated weight training and developed weight machines at a time when the medical profession discouraged such regimens, warning that athletes would become musclebound, women would look like men, the elderly could suffer heart attacks, and everyone would lose their sex drive. Undaunted, he persisted. In 1951, he launched the first full-time exercise program on television, *The Jack LaLanne Show.* In those early days, he couldn't find sponsors, so he created his own nutritional products to sell, including the first breakfast nutrition drink, "Instant Breakfast."

Today, of course, it's a different story. A world of physical fitness experts has followed LaLanne's lead, and he's a fitness icon lauded by millions of all ages. His machines are considered state of the art, and his first health club—which became a nationwide chain—today is Bally's. Along with his wife, Elaine, 81, LaLanne has helped tens of thousands of people throughout the years who are living proof that the right approach to living and fitness promotes a long, healthy life.

Baby boomer and nationally respected retirement planning expert Rettick, 54, has spent decades helping thousands of people understand what it takes to get fiscally fit and stay that way. A recognized leader in his industry, he's an investment advisor representative with Brookstone Capital Management and a licensed insurance agent. An in-demand national speaker, he's also a leader in the life insurance industry, and founder and CEO of Covenant Reliance Producers LLC, a Nashville, Tennessee-based organization that trains advisors on retirement issues and essential solutions important to soon-to-be retirees and current retirees.

Rettick, a father of four with 13 grandchildren, also knows firsthand much of the pain, heartache, and devastation that occurs when an elderly person isn't financially fit. In the late 1980s, he watched his family struggle with his grandparents' "unexpected" illnesses and the subsequent financial strain. He saw the assets that his grandparents had worked their lives to accumulate swallowed up by nursing-home and medical bills. That's when he made the commitment to work with retirees to help them plan financially so that they and their families could avoid similar hardships and suffering.

Subsequently, Rettick has become *the* expert on retirement and financial planning, with access to the entire universe of investment vehicles and options. Rettick successfully blends financial vehicles such as fixed annuities, mutual funds, exchange traded funds, long-term-care insurance policies, life insurance, and more. Rettick creates customized solutions that match his individual client's personal goals and financial profiles, helping ensure that a retiree's assets last an entire lifetime.

Together, LaLanne and Rettick have a prescription for your fitness—physical and fiscal. This book isn't about programs and processes doomed to failure. We're not going to order you to do this and only this, then buy that, and more. You don't need to spend a fortune on costly exercise equipment or expensive diet supplements, on fat financial consultant commissions, or questionable investments.

Instead, ours is a program for physical and fiscal fitness that's doable, dependable, and nets concrete, recognizable, and satisfying results today and tomorrow. Plus, we're here as an ongoing resource for you.

This program isn't about depriving you or your loved ones of food or funds. But you do have to learn how to make the most of what you have, physically and financially, and be aware of what you do in terms of risks and rewards in the near-term and the long run.

The book is divided into three parts to make it easier to follow:

- Part I—Physical Fitness/Financial Fitness: The Perfect Fit
- Part II—Physical Fitness for a Lifetime
- Part III—Financial Fitness for Your Future

At the end of each chapter is a *Roadmap to Success* that details important points to remember—for specific age groups, too, when applicable—as well as *More Resources,* which lists additional related resources. Throughout, pull-outs and tips will help you better understand your own situation, as well as provide proven words of encouragement to help you get going and stay on track. This book is, after all, about motivating you to get physically and fiscally fit for the rest of your life!

LaLanne said it best back in 1952: *Get off your seat and onto your feet.*

So let's get started now. (Good luck! Let us know how you're doing, too. E-mail us at **info@mattandjack.com**.)

PART I

Physical Fitness/

Financial Fitness:

The Perfect Fit

Chapter 1

Get Fit: Why Bother?

Stop for a moment and think about how you feel today. Whatever your age, do you have any aches or pains, chronic illnesses, or limitations? Do you move around a lot? Do you exercise? Or are you rather sedentary? Are you overweight or underweight? Do you ever worry about your future health or that of a loved one?

Do you worry about how you'll pay off today's bills and fund tomorrow's expenses? Do you have an aging family member or loved one who struggles to pay or worries about paying, for his or her care now or in the near future? Do you worry that you'll find yourself in the same situation? Worse yet, has that loved one been forced into poverty in order to qualify for Medicaid to pay for nursing-home expenses?

For many of us, these questions don't have simple answers. Yet we all need to ask and answer them honestly. This book is, after all, about helping you and your loved ones get on track financially and physically to improve your lives now and for the future. So even if your situation is less than optimal, take heart. If you're concerned about your future finances or tomorrow's health, you're far from alone. The good news is that you can start to build fitness—whether physical or financial—right now. It's never too late to reverse the tide of neglect, and even baby steps lead to giant rewards. If you don't take steps today to make a difference in your life and that of your loved ones, you aren't immune to what may happen in the future.

If you're still not convinced that you should act to make changes today, let's look more closely at what's really happening with the health and future finances of most Americans.

Sobering Statistics

Chances are we all have a few aches and pains, physically and financially, because, unfortunately, most Americans are neither physically nor financially fit. In fact, the United States is in a health and financial crisis, leaving most Americans ill-prepared for the future.

Compounding the problem, the first of the nation's 76 million baby boomers are heading into retirement and looking to an already severely stressed Medicare and Social Security system for help. Every day more than 6,000 Americans celebrate their 65th birthday (Alliance for Aging Research, *Independence for Older Americans*). By 2030, almost one out of every five Americans—approximately 72 million people—will be age 65 and older (U.S. Census Bureau, *65+ in the United States: 2005*).

Let's look at a few more dollars and cents of aging:

- A big chunk of Americans worry they'll barely make it financially in retirement, or are afraid they'll simply outlive their money. Almost one in four (24 percent) baby boomers—those born 1946 to 1964—say they expect to have just enough money in retirement for basic living expenses, while another 17 percent say they won't even be able to handle that. Among the already retired, another 25 percent say they'll just meet basic expenses, with another 12 percent unable to do so (Pew Research Center survey; "Baby Boomers: From the Age of Aquarius to the Age of Responsibility," December 2005).

- More than 46 million Americans under age 65 were without health insurance in 2005 (Kaiser Commission on Medicaid and the Uninsured, "The Uninsured: A Primer—Key Facts About Americans Without Health Insurance," *www.kaiserfamilyfoundation.org/uninsured/upload/7451-021.pdf*), The Henry J. Kaiser Family Foundation, October 2006. The information was reprinted with permission from the Henry J. Kaiser Family Foundation. The Kaiser Family foundation, based in Menlo Park, California, is a nonprofit, private operating foundation focusing on the major healthcare issues facing the nation and is not associated with Kaiser Permanente or Kaiser Industries).

- In the year 2000 alone, spending on healthcare in the United States totaled an estimated $1.3 trillion. That's the most of any industrialized country in the world (National Center for Health Statistics).

- More than 1.8 million people are in nursing homes today.

- The 2007 national average daily rate for a semi-private room in a nursing home is $189 ($68,985 annually), a $6 or 3.3 % increase over the 2006 rate of $183 (The MetLife Market Survey of Nursing Home & Home Care Costs, October 2007).

- The national average hourly rate for a home healthcare aide is $19, which remains the same as the 2006 average. The 2007 national average hourly homemaker/companion rate is $18, which represents a $1 increase over last year's average (*The MetLife Market Survey of Adult Day Services & Home Care Costs*, September 2007).

It's no wonder Americans fret about future finances as they age, and that so many go broke when faced with funding their care. That's because, contrary to popular belief, Medicare does not pay for extended long-term care, and Medicaid, the equivalent of medical welfare, will pay for your care only if you're basically broke. (More on that in Part III of this book.) In fact, Medicaid is the primary source of payment for 58 percent of nursing-home residents. ("Medicaid and Long-Term Care," #7089, The Henry J. Kaiser Family Foundation, May 2004.)

(Un)Health Issues

Thanks to medical breakthroughs, Americans of today are living longer. That means they're retired longer, and their money must last longer too.

Workdays of Your Life

The average person spends approximately 12,262 days of his or her life working.

Average work span: From age 18 to 67, or 49 years × 250 days a year (assuming a five-day workweek and 2 weeks off for vacation).

Total: 12,262 days (including an additional 12 days for leap years).

The average female is retired for almost 3,400 days (ages 67 to 80) and a male, just more than 1,825 days (ages 67 to 74). This longer life, however, doesn't always translate to higher quality of life. Consider a few more sobering statistics, this time on the state of Americans' physical fitness.

- 80 percent of older Americans live with at least one chronic condition, and 50 percent with at least two (Centers for Disease Control and Prevention. "Public Health and Aging: Trends in Aging—United States and Worldwide," *MMWR* 2003; 52 (06): 101–106).

- At age 65 a person has at least a 40 percent chance of needing nursing-home care sometime during his or her lifetime, and a 10 percent chance that the stay will be five years or longer. At age 85, the odds climb to 55 percent (U.S. Department of Health and Human Services).

There are, however, some promising health statistics for the elderly. The percentage of Americans age 65 who have a disability dropped to 19.7 percent in 1999, from 26.2 percent in 1982. Heart disease deaths have dropped too, according to the 2005 Census report, *65+ in the United States*. (The report was prepared by the National Institute on Aging in the National Institutes of Health at the U.S. Department of Health and Human Services.) Still, the overall picture isn't pretty.

Unprepared Masses

Disheartened by the numbers? We're not done yet! As bad as those numbers are, few people prepare for the realities they reflect. Consider that fewer than 10 percent of Americans have long-term-care insurance. Eight in 10 fail to have a long-term-care plan of any kind simply because they don't think they need one, they don't get around to it, they don't think they can afford it, or they don't believe they qualify for anything. Far too many elderly also end up on Medicaid and struggling because they think that's their only alternative.

Those elderly are mistaken. Financially, you don't have to be broke, resort to welfare, and rely on the mercy of others for care as you age. Physically, you don't have to be overweight, out of shape, and unable to help yourself either. If you take the right steps today and plan for tomorrow, your golden years needn't be only a tarnished dream. You do have choices, and lots of them.

Andrew, 76, learned that lesson the hard way—fortunately, before it was too late. He realized he had choices after spending down only a small portion of his and his wife's $200,000 in retirement savings.

Andrew's wife, 72, had Alzheimer's disease, and was in a nursing home. She didn't qualify for Medicaid, so Andrew paid $6,000 a month out of pocket for her care. Desperate to turn off the money spigot and afraid the couple's small nest egg would run out long before the need for it did, at a friend's urging he attended a Matt Rettick Successful Retirement Strategies Workshop in Nashville, Tennessee. The decision turned into an eye-opener and a life-changing experience. "This sounds like a commercial," says Andrew, "but I couldn't believe how little effort it took on my part, and how easy it was to really change my financial future and give me peace of mind about it all too."

We'll go into the details later, but basically, Andrew learned about reallocating ownership of assets, and the benefits of fixed annuities converted into a monthly income stream. The couple's assets and income were reallocated to the non-nursing home spouse, Andrew, so that his wife qualified for Medicaid (in fact, Medicaid began picking up the nursing-home costs the very next month!). Prior to applying for Medicaid on behalf of his wife, Andrew purchased a Medicaid-friendly annuity with a single premium or lump sum that began to pay him an immediate monthly revenue stream. These financial moves cost him almost no extra money other than the single payment for the annuity, and he experienced immediate emotional relief, and, almost as quickly, financial relief.

It sounds too good to be true, but in this case, it isn't. The reason: Not enough people recognize the financial options they have to fund long-term care. It's never too late to start either, as Andrew's case shows. Andrew took the time, got the proper guidance, and learned the right steps to take to preserve his future. It's time for you, similar to Andrew, to take charge of your financial health today.

Health and Finances Intertwined

Worries about money affect your physical being too. If you're not sure about that, consider this: Have you ever lost sleep because of money—perhaps while trying to figure out how to pay for something, stewing over a late or forgotten bill, or just rationalizing an expense? If your sleep is always sound and immediate, you're in the minority. When Andrew was paying out $6,000 a month, he constantly worried about not only his wife's future, but his as well. He lost weight he couldn't afford to lose. He seemed to catch every cold, and his children fretted constantly about his declining health. Once his financial picture and his outlook on life improved, he bounced back to his old self (more on the value of positive thinking from Jack LaLanne in Chapter 5).

Even if the solution to your financial woes isn't as simple as Andrew's, dealing with them is easier if you're physically fit.

> *Your bank account and your health account are synonymous. The more you put in, the more you can take out.*
>
> —*Jack LaLanne*

You have to be physically fit to truly be mentally fit, and you must be mentally fit to get yourself financially fit. If you doubt that, try this exercise: Take the middle finger of your left hand and bend it back as far as you can. Really pull it. Feel the pain? Now imagine trying to make sound financial decisions while you're in that kind of pain—or worse. It would be pretty tough, wouldn't it?

That's just one big reason we all have to start with physical health. The other: If you're healthy and physically fit, you may never need long-term care in a nursing home, your home, or anywhere else. You won't end up obese and at risk, sickly, and helpless.

A big LaLanne-ism: "Exercise is king; nutrition is queen. Put them together and you have a kingdom." Add a little forward-thinking financial planning, and that kingdom will have a rosy future too. That's a Rettick-ism!

Often-Ignored Road

Of course, ideally we should all get started early with fitness, both physically and financially. We need to exercise, eat right, and develop the habit of saving, as well as planning ahead. Unfortunately, life rarely happens that way. Instead, we generally take a haphazard approach that tends to focus on today rather than tomorrow. The modus operandi: "Why worry? I won't need a nursing home or long-term care."

Well, statistics show there's a good chance you will!

Most of us spend our early years struggling to get ahead, perhaps starting a family, working long hours, and playing as though there's no tomorrow. We find it difficult to carve out personal time for exercise, reflection, or studied nutrition, and nearly impossible to sock away money for the future. As we age, and, for many of us, our children grow older, the go-go-go pace revs up. Instead of emphasizing proper nutrition, we eat on the go, with "meals" sandwiched between our work, the sitter, and shuttling ourselves or the kids to soccer, baseball, or the sport du jour, to piano, dance, tae kwan do, and other activities. Often we eat in the car, gulping bites at stoplights. No wonder fast food is a favorite. (It's also a killer for your diet, your health, and maybe, ultimately, your life. More on that in Chapter 4.) Fast food is convenient and easy, but there's a price to pay for everything. Most of these drive-by food fixes are fried and overcooked, and high in cholesterol and calories. As a result, they add unwanted pounds and can make you feel lazy and lethargic.

The same live-for-today philosophy pervades the way we handle our finances. Ours, after all, is an immediate-gratification society. Instead of putting that holiday bonus into a retirement savings vehicle, it goes toward the home entertainment center. That raise makes the payments on the shiny new SUV. And that long-term-care insurance policy the neighbor suggested? We can put that off until later—much later. Saving becomes even more unlikely for those with elderly parents who often bear the financial and physical burdens of helping them.

It's time for all of us to step off the merry-go-round and wake up to the reality that we need to eat right and save right. If we don't, we'll pay the ultimate price. Compare your body to a car. Take care of it, do routine maintenance, and provide the right fuel, and it will last a long time. Ignore scheduled maintenance and fill the gas tank with water, and it won't make it out of the driveway.

Real-Life Stories

Fitness guru LaLanne didn't start out as a specimen of physical perfection. Instead, growing up in California, he hit a low point on a sugar high, until he attended a lecture by pioneer nutritionist Paul Bragg, who talked about the benefits of diet and exercise. That lecture changed LaLanne's diet and his life. He studied all he could about nutrition, fitness, and the human body. He became a convert to healthy eating and exercise, graduated from chiropractic college, and the rest is decades of well-documented history.

LaLanne's dad, on the other hand, like many Americans, never woke up to the benefits of healthy eating and exercise. He committed suicide with his knife and fork, says LaLanne, referring to his dad's preferences for high-fat foods such as cheese, meats, and butter. He died at a young age. That contrasts with his mother, who saw the healthy change in her son and joined him in his program of exercise and nutrition. Despite early years of very poor health, she lived to the spry old age of 94! "Because of the change in her eating habits, she added at least 20 to 25 years to her lifespan," says LaLanne. "On the other hand, Dad took about 25 years off his life because of his lifestyle and his eating habits."

> *Everything we do in life is a matter of habit. Habits make you what you are. My mother just took a few bad habits and exchanged them for good habits. My dad didn't change any of his habits, and look what happened to him.*
>
> *—Jack LaLanne*

Financial planning expert Matt Rettick didn't start out financially healthy either. In fact, he too hit a low point before taking charge and accomplishing fiscal fitness. His low point came in the early 1990s when, with a $50,000 line of credit, mounting credit-card debt, a mortgage payment that was two months behind and in the early stages of foreclosure, and two car payments, he jumped off the merry-go-round. "We were sick and tired of being sick and tired," he says. "I got radical. We stopped buying things on credit and started paying off one debt at a time."

> *We just got tired of being a slave to our lender.*
>
> *—Matt Rettick*

As Rettick's finances began to improve, so did his confidence that he could achieve financial security. "The day we became debt-free, I was ecstatic. It took six months until we really realized we didn't have to pay the mortgage!"

How can you get as physically and fiscally fit as LaLanne and Rettick? Simple—pay attention to how you treat your body and what you do with your money. Forgo the instant gratification. Do you really need that hot fudge sundae or hot Internet stock? Instead, invest physically and financially for the long haul through physical exercise and fiscal discipline.

Robert and Marie refused to acknowledge these realities. Robert adores colas, chips, beer, and beef, and all of it in vast quantities. He is 5 feet 8 inches tall, but weighs 280 pounds, has gout, and constantly complains of sore feet. He blames his feet on poor shoes and insists he's not fat, just "solid."

Marie opts for wine instead of beer and eats a bit more fish than beef, yet still enjoys junk food and is overweight by about 35 pounds. Both constantly complain of ill health. Although only in their 50s, their insurance rates are high, and both have slowed considerably. They also have no long-term-care health plan or insurance.

Tom, 39, woke up to health and fitness, literally, while watching late-night reruns of the hit fitness show, *The Jack LaLanne Show*. He picked up on the message of healthy eating and exercise, dropped those stubborn 30 extra pounds, and now proudly talks about how much better he looks and feels. All that's left is to get his finances in a little better long-term order.

Isabelle, now 67, became a convert to health and fitness after her husband died a number of years earlier. He had had no life insurance and left her with a mountain of unpaid bills. Meanwhile, she received only a small paycheck as a receptionist. Worried about her physical and financial security, Isabelle looked into long-term-care insurance (more on that later in the book), but couldn't afford it on her meager income. So good health became her way of hedging her bets on ever needing long-term care.

Widowed, Louise, 55, is self-employed, has two grown children, and lives alone with her two dogs in a small town in Ohio. Her children and their families live across the country. In average health, Louise opted to take out a long-term-care insurance policy (with an inflation increase built in). The reason, she says, was concern that she not burden her kids with her care in the event that something happened to her. It's a financial squeeze for her, but she bit the bullet, cut back on her travel and entertainment, and pays the approximately $1,670 a year premium. The peace of mind, she says, is well worth it. "I no longer lose sleep over the 'what if.'"

Let's take a closer look at what Louise is paying and what it might buy her. Let's say Louise lives another 25 years, and continues to pay her $1,670 every year until she dies or needs the benefits. Although premiums aren't absolutely locked in, they are expected to stay level once the policy is purchased, according to nationally recognized industry analyst and consultant Claude Thau, president of Overland Park, Kansas-based Thau Inc. That means Louise probably will pay throughout the years a total of $41,750. But if she needed long-term-care insurance, say, at age 80, her policy could pay up to nearly $122,000 in benefits that year, and more in the following years.

Not a bad investment, especially considering that today's national average cost of just one year in a nursing home is almost $70,000.

More Details

Risk. Lack of physical and fiscal fitness is all about risk. If you don't get healthy, you risk physical complications and may die prematurely. If you don't prepare for the future financially, you risk having no control or money, or becoming a burden to your family or the system. But how much risk is acceptable for you?

That's your decision. This book is all about helping you make the right choices for your own unique situation. Louise was willing to accept only minimal risk when it came to her future long-term-care needs. The much-younger Tom decided to hedge his bets and get in physical shape early.

Whatever you decide about risk, it starts with understanding what the real risk is. Is it your health, or that of your loved ones? Is it your money, or that of your spouse, loved ones, or heirs?

Figuring out those answers means taking stock of who depends on you, as well as assessing your eating and exercise habits, physical condition, genetics, family history, and propensity for certain diseases. It also involves recognizing what's at stake with a particular investment or strategy, and the repercussions of each. Let's look more closely at financial risk.

Ideally, we all want to have the right amount of money at the right time, and for the right length of time. (We'll go into the details on how to help you do that in Chapter 6.) A financial goal, for example, could be to have the last check you write before you die bounce!

Changing Demographics. The good news is that just because you retire or turn 65 doesn't mean you're automatically ailing, out to pasture as far as work, or relegated to the front porch for your later years. Increasing numbers of Americans are waking up to better health and fitness, and view age 65 not as retirement but as a signal to change careers, alter lifestyles, travel, and more. In fact, even the federal government is phasing in its official retirement age to 67.

All this translates into more time to make your money work for you and to get in shape and enjoy life. It's a new retirement these days, one with infinite possibilities and the potential for tremendous enjoyment.

In case you still think 65 is the command to sit down and slow down, consider just one of LaLanne's Herculean feats of strength and stamina *after* age 65: In 1984, at age 70, handcuffed, shackled, and fighting strong winds and currents, he towed 70 boats with 70 people from the Queen's Way Bridge in the Long Beach Harbor to the Queen Mary 1 1/2 miles away!

> *People don't die of old age; they die of neglect.*
>
> —*Jack LaLanne*

Roadmap to Success

Making the time to be physically and fiscally fit today will help keep you that way for many tomorrows to come. If you're healthy and in shape, you've automatically reduced your odds of contracting a chronic illness and possibly needing future care. But just in case you do require care—and chances are you may—plan ahead now. It will give you and your loved ones peace of mind to enjoy that newfound health to live your life to the fullest. Beyond forced poverty or debilitating financial and emotional stress for you and your loved ones, you *do* have options if you plan ahead.

What should you do today? The first step is to contact a qualified financial advisor with specific expertise in aging issues. Also, consider the following:

- If you're not yet retired, capitalize on the financial power of compounding to get financially fit, and make a difference in your future health too—get into nutrition and a healthy lifestyle now.

- Start planning now. The longer you wait to get in shape physically, the more difficult it may be. And from a financial point of view, you need to get your affairs in order and make contingency plans for the possibility of long-term care *now*.

- If you think you're starting to "feel your age," get up and get going. Mobility usually translates to freedom as you age.

More Resources

- Covenant Consumer Resource Center (*www .covenantresource.com*): A consumer-oriented Website from Matt Rettick dedicated to helping pre-retirees and retirees access the necessary information to safeguard their estates and become financially fit for life. Check out the free booklets available on a variety of topics.

- Eat 5 to 9 Servings of Fruits and Vegetables a Day for Better Health (*www.5aday.gov*): From the U.S. Department of Health and Human Services, National Institutes of Health, and National Cancer Institute, the site includes plenty of information on good nutrition and health.

- Employee Benefit Research Institute (*www.ebri.org*): Private, nonprofit research group that focuses on health, savings, retirement, and economic security issues, with plenty of facts, figures, and studies that better inform consumers.

- Jack LaLanne (*www.jacklalanne.com*): The official Website of health and fitness icon Jack LaLanne, it includes information and products to help you eat right, get fit, and stay that way.

- MyMoney.gov (*www.mymoney.gov*): From the U.S. National Literacy and Education Commission, this is a free resource on money matters ranging from savings and investing to life events and retirement planning.

- National Council on the Aging (*www.ncoa.org*): A national nonprofit that's dedicated to improving the health and independence of older people. The site includes information on health, research, advocacy, Medicare, and more; check out its Center for Healthy Aging at *www.healthyagingprograms .org*, and click on "Health Topics."

- National Institutes of Health (*health.nih.gov*): From the U.S. Department of Health and Human Services and NIH, this site has information on health, healthy lifestyles, illnesses, and more.

- President's Council on Physical Fitness and Sports (*www.fitness.gov*): This is an advisory committee of volunteer citizens who advise the president through the Secretary of Health and Human Services about physical activity, fitness, and sports in America. Click on "Resources" for help, information, and tools on physical fitnessand check out The President's Challenge (*www.presidentschallenge.org*) for more valuable tools and to find out more about getting fit.

Chapter 2

Critical Decisions Now:

Financial, Legal, and

End-of-Life

The right legal documents help ensure your care and that of your loved ones.

—*Matt Rettick*

Getting fit financially is rooted in being prepared. That means having financial wherewithal, and the right plans in place when you need them. It also means making sure you have the legal documentation necessary to carry out the plans you've put together.

One old gentleman meticulously planned every detail of distributing his assets. He even went to the trouble and expense of setting up an irrevocable trust to help ensure that his wishes were carried out and to cut down on his estate's tax liability, as well as speed up the distribution process after his death (more on that later). There was only one problem: After he died, it was discovered that he had forgotten to fill out the necessary documentation and paperwork to formally transfer any assets into the trust. This overlooked detail was of such significance that it torpedoed his entire plan.

Then there's the case of Terri Schiavo. Remember, she was the young Florida woman who had no living will and was kept alive via feeding tubes in an arguably vegetative state for years while her husband and her parents fought over what to do with her. Schiavo's husband claimed his wife never would have wanted to be kept alive through artificial means. Her parents took the opposite view. Schiavo's husband's side eventually prevailed, and Terri was disconnected from the feeding tube, and died, but not before an acrimonious, protracted battle. Terri Schiavo had never taken the time to fill out the documentation that would have made her wishes known and spared her family much heartache.

When Helen was diagnosed with a terminal illness, she talked to her daughter, Rachel, about having her body cremated after she died. The disposition of her mother's body was not something Rachel had thought about, and she never would have considered cremation an option. But Helen was very specific that cremation was her choice, so Rachel promised to make sure her mother's wishes were honored. Unfortunately, Helen never wrote down her wishes in the form of a funeral directive. When she died, her husband refused to believe that Helen had specifically requested to be cremated. A family battle ensued, and not until a sobbing and near-hysterical Rachel threatened to boycott the funeral of her beloved mother did the father finally give in. The emotional situation easily could have been avoided if only the right documentation—even if it's not legally binding—had been in place.

No matter our age, we all need to make sure we don't overlook putting down certain details in writing. Let's look more closely at a few of those pieces of paper that can make an enormous difference in the quality of life and death for ourselves and our loved ones.

Will

A will conveys how you would like your assets, your property, and your possessions distributed after your death. It specifies who gets what, and, if you choose, why. No matter our age, we all need to have a formal last will and testament that's signed, witnessed, notarized, *and* put in a safe place. Better still, put several signed, witnessed, and notarized copies in *several* places other than a safe deposit box that's automatically sealed on your death.

If you die without a will, that's called dying "intestate." The state then comes in and distributes your estate according to a strict property-distribution formula. If you always promised that Renoir painting to your old college roommate, you better have a formal will stating such, or your old roommate is out of luck. Under the state formula, your assets are divided among family based on a strict hierarchy.

If it matters to you who gets what among your assets after you die, be specific in your will. Even the friendliest, most loving family can get ugly when it comes to assets and heirs.

If you've lived with a companion for many years, but the two of you never married, and you would like him or her to have your home, be assured that's not likely to happen unless you have a formal will that very specifically stipulates your bequest. Don't count on the benevolence of family members either. People tend to do funny things after someone dies, especially when money is involved.

Your will should also stipulate an executor and backup executor for your estate. They are the person and alternate who will oversee the closing of your estate and distribution of your assets. Choose carefully, though. Is your executor someone who will be evenhanded and fair? Is it someone who is committed to fulfilling your wishes? Is it someone who is honest? The answers to those questions aren't always easy to discern, and the best choice isn't always a family member or a close friend. Often, an attorney or other legal or financial advisor may be a solid, unbiased agent to carry out your wishes. Or if you still would like to or need to have a family member as executor, even if he or she has a vested interest, you may want to consider naming an unbiased and independent third party—that advisor, perhaps—as a co-executor to bring the element of fairness into the handling of your affairs.

Pay attention to the laws relating to wills and property transfer in the different states where you may hold assets. Those laws can vary, and what suffices as documentation in one state may not be considered adequate in another.

If you have children who are minors, an adult dependent child with a disability, or a dependent loved one who needs care, your will should also include a guardianship provision that addresses who will care for that person. It's generally a good idea to name one person directly responsible for the person's care, and someone else in charge of the finances you set aside, usually in an irrevocable trust, for that dependent.

Trusts and More

Whether or not you have a dependent minor, you still may want to consider placing some or all of your assets in some kind of trust. You don't need to have a lot of money or assets for a trust to make sense either.

A trust is a legal vehicle that holds certain assets for the benefit of someone or something. A trust can be *living*, which means it takes effect while the grantor (or person setting up the trust) is still alive, or *testamentary*, which means it goes into effect after that person dies. If it's *irrevocable*, it's a separate legal entity that cannot be changed once it goes into effect, and its assets are removed from its grantor's assets. If it's *revocable*, those assets remain part of the grantor's assets and are still under his or her control.

As we've mentioned, an irrevocable trust is an excellent tool to ensure financial support for a young child or a family member with a disability. It can be set up while you're alive, or as a testamentary trust as stipulated in your will after you die. An irrevocable trust not only removes its assets from your estate, but it also bypasses the potential delays of probate after your death and keeps your affairs private.

A revocable living trust is a way to plan for the contingencies of your care and your affairs in the event that you become unable to manage your affairs yourself. As the trustee, the person in charge of the trust, you remain in full control of the trust as long as you are able, but if something happens to you, your named successor trustee can take over responsibility for your affairs. A revocable living trust also avoids the delays of probate, disbursing the assets in the trust after you die with minimal hassle and delay.

A trust also can be a way to ensure a loved one's financial well-being after your death. Melinda, 84, had been married to George for 39 years, so she knew well his tendencies to fritter away money on frivolous and ridiculous inventions and ventures—everything from the automatic manhole cover for city streets to the $39.95 late-night special on TV that did absolutely nothing but break instantly.

That's why she always kept certain assets and equities separate from George's as a kind of insurance policy in case he lost everything.

That's also why, when she became terminally ill, she arranged with her attorney to set up a testamentary trust (it went into effect on her death as stipulated in her will) to be funded with her modest equities portfolio. The trust, under the guidance of the trustee, her attorney, would then pay George a regular income from its income or the principal, if necessary. In essence, Melinda was dictating her wishes from beyond the grave.

Trust Basics

Many different types of trusts are available to meet various financial, emotional, physical, and health needs. A few trust basics include:

Trust: *Legal entity that holds certain assets for the benefit of someone or something.*

Grantor: *Individual who establishes the trust.*

Trustee: *Individual named in the trust to manage it and make decisions relating to it.*

Living Trust: *Goes into effect while the grantor is still alive.*

Testamentary Trust: *Takes effect when the grantor dies.*

Irrevocable Trust: *Separate legal entity that cannot be changed once it's in effect; its assets belong solely to the trust, which files its own tax return.*

Revocable Trust: *Grantor can change it at any time; its control remains with the grantor, who can act as trustee; its assets remain part of the grantor's assets.*

Trusts, no matter what kind, can be complicated to set up correctly, so it's best to work with a qualified attorney. Remember the elderly gentleman who set up a trust himself and forgot to fund it? (That scenario is not so far-fetched, either, and happens more often than you would think!) Professional legal assistance undeniably adds cost to the process, but the peace of mind from knowing that your wishes will be carried out and will stand up to legal challenges that may surface after your death, is well worth the extra expense.

Keep in mind too that trust details and documents need to be revisited periodically to make sure they're up to date, especially if you or a trust beneficiary has experienced any major life changes such as births, deaths, marriages, divorces, or the like, and as laws change.

More Options

If you prefer not to spend the extra time or money to set up a trust, and truly feel you don't need one, a quick, no-extra-cost way to disburse an asset such as a bank account or certificate of deposit after your death is by making it payable on death, up front, to a beneficiary. Then all that your heir needs to do after your death is provide proof of your death, usually in the form of a certified copy of the death certificate, and the asset is his or hers—no hassles, no waiting.

Life insurance policies with named beneficiaries offer the same kind of fast, efficient disbursement to heirs after someone's death. Usually all it takes is a brief call to the insurance company to start the disbursement process

Another option that can smooth the transfer of a major property asset such as a home is to title the house in joint tenancy with right of survivorship with an heir. The deed or title to the property is proof of the transfer. But keep in mind that it's generally *not* a good idea to include your children's or grandchildren's names on your assets, because you could be held liable and your assets at risk if a child has legal issues. For example, if the child gets involved in a divorce, owes back taxes, or faces a lawsuit, your nest egg is fair game too. Instead, consider a payable-on-death or beneficiary designation for IRAs, life insurance, and annuities.

Asset Designations

You also need to make sure that the heirs designated on your various assets—bank accounts, money-market accounts, property deeds, houses, boats, horses, cars, IRAs, CDs, old pension plans, insurance policies (even that small policy from two employers ago)—are correct. Often people forget to change a beneficiary designation when they switch jobs, change partners, or when someone dies. Beyond a simple beneficiary designation, you may want to consider special designations for various assets. Transfer on death (TOD) or payable on death (POD), for example, often are excellent approaches with bank and brokerage accounts, certificates of deposit, and more. Both enable you to designate that a particular asset or assets pass immediately to the named beneficiary. Another option is to place assets in a revocable living trust. The assets in that trust remain fully in your control as its trustee as long as you're able to make decisions yourself. However, if you become incapacitated and can't make decisions for yourself, or after you die, the trust is administered by your designated successor trustee. This can be an excellent way to ensure control of your finances while you're alive as well as after you're dead.

While getting physically and fiscally fit, be sure to check up on all those old designations and update the beneficiaries to reflect your current wishes and circumstances. Otherwise, that ex-husband who dumped you and whom you now can't stand could end up with an unexpected infusion of your hard-earned cash should you die before him. Or what about that once bright and shining, full-of-potential nephew who made some poor choices and now is in trouble with the law? If you didn't formally, in writing, remove his name as beneficiary on that $10,000 certificate of deposit you bought four years ago, it's his, and it's his to do with as he pleases, should something happen to you.

Power of Attorney for Finances

No matter your age, you should designate someone to have power of attorney for your finances in case you become incapacitated and can't handle your affairs yourself. In the case of a married couple, you would likely want to name your spouse as the next person in line to make financial decisions for you if you can't. But what if your spouse isn't the best choice to make financial decisions, or if he or she becomes incapacitated along with you—you're both in an automobile accident, for example? You therefore would want to elect an alternate to act on your behalf. Don't overlook designating alternates for your initial power of attorney designee.

The power of attorney can be designated as *durable*, which goes into effect as soon as it's signed and remains in effect should you become incapacitated, and until you die or the courts remove the power. Or the power can be *springing*, which goes into effect only when you are declared incompetent, or some other event occurs as named in the document. The benefit of a durable power is that it's automatically there if and when you unexpectedly need it; the drawback is that the named individual actually could take over control of your assets immediately. With a springing power, however, the details of what constitutes your "incompetence" can get a bit sticky.

People often give a trusted financial or legal advisor durable financial power of attorney; the document will be signed and then put away until it's needed. That's one reason why it's so important to name a trusted individual, and even an alternate or two as backup in the event that your original choice is not available or decides he or she doesn't want to make those decisions. The power of attorney must be durable so that the power stays in force.

Durable Power of Attorney for Healthcare

Just as you should name a trusted individual to handle your financial affairs in the event that you can't, you also should name someone to handle your healthcare decisions. One does not and cannot automatically handle the other unless legal documentation stipulates that.

The durable power of attorney for healthcare goes by a variety of names, including *healthcare proxy* and *healthcare agent.* You choose this individual to make health and medical decisions for you if you can't. As with the power of attorney for finance, you must name the person you would like to take over. The duty does *not* automatically fall to a spouse if no one else is named. Again, it's a good idea to have an alternate or two listed as backup. The auto-accident scenario in which you and your spouse are both injured applies here too. Also, if you're in a medical crisis, your loved one most likely is in the midst of an emotionally draining crisis too, and may not be the best person to make difficult life-and-death medical decisions for you. A less emotionally involved backup person may be in a much better position to make rational choices.

Living Will

This is a legal document that states your wishes regarding being kept alive by artificial means.

Remember the Terri Schiavo case we mentioned earlier? She was in her late 20s when hit by a massive stroke. If Schiavo had had a signed, notarized living will, it would have stipulated without a reasonable doubt her wishes with regard to life support in the event that something happened to her.

Something can happen to you too, at any age. Do you want to force those gut-wrenching life-and-death decisions on a loved one? Do you want to be kept alive by artificial means? You should address these questions and decide the answers for yourself, rather than leaving them for your loved ones to wrestle with.

Be specific about what you would like done or not done to prolong your life by artificial means. That includes spelling out your wishes regarding artificial nutrition and hydration, and pain control. This is your opportunity to make these decisions for yourself, as opposed to leaving them to others if you become incapacitated.

Note: Keep several signed and notarized copies of this document in readily available places, including with your physician or healthcare professional. A living will does no good if it's locked up and inaccessible in a safety deposit box.

Do-Not-Resuscitate Order

If you do not want to be resuscitated in the event of a massive heart attack or some other respiratory failure, you will need more than a living will. In an emergency, if an ambulance is summoned to your home, the emergency medical technicians will do their very best and use all possible means to revive or resuscitate you—no matter your age or physical condition, and whether you have a living will or not—unless you have a do-not-resuscitate order.

Funeral Directive

Willy had been to enough funerals in his life. In fact, he was so tired of them that he decided all he wanted when he died was to be buried quietly with a handful of close family attending. And instead of what he referred to as a "reception of dull people moping around" over his death, Willy decided he wanted a party held in his honor, in absentia, of course. So he lay down the rules in a funeral directive and wrote a blank check to his country club for the party. He detailed the event in writing, including the guests, the entertainment, the food, the decorations, and more. After he died, he was toasted again and again at a heck of a party, with decidedly no "moping around."

Trish also had very specific ideas on what she wanted to happen to her body after she died, and on the kind of funeral she wanted. She wasn't religious, and especially didn't want any church services, because she thought that would be hypocritical. But she only talked about her wishes. She never took the time to get her preferences on paper in the form of a funeral directive. Her family tried their best to decide what she would have wanted, but the affair ended up being held in a church, and was a far cry from what Trish would have liked.

Funeral directives aren't legally binding documents, but they provide a way for you to have input on that ultimate, final episode of your life on Earth. They also ease the hardship and pain of grieving loved ones by relieving them of some tough decisions.

Decisions about everything from caskets to cremation, flowers, burial plots, headstones, and more, can take a financial as well as emotional toll on loved ones. Often we spend far more than necessary or even prudent on the after-death details for a loved one simply because poor decisions are made in a time of stress.

Roadmap to Success

The details are in the documents. No matter your age, it's important to make sure that you have written down, signed, notarized, and put in a safe place those documents necessary to help ensure that your wishes are carried out in life and in death. Without the appropriate documents, you and/or your loved ones can end up devastated emotionally, physically, and financially. So why not take care of those details today? Imagine the sense of freedom you'll feel when those "should-do" documents are finally off your plate.

Here are a few of the important documents and issues to consider (not all may be applicable to your individual situation):

- A will (with guardianship provision—including financial support—for dependents if applicable.
- Living will.
- Do-not-resuscitate order, if that's your desire.

- Durable or springing power of attorney for finances, and durable power of attorney for healthcare.
- Various types of trusts, especially if practical to ensure smooth transfer of your estate.

More Resources

- Aging With Dignity (*www.agingwithdignity.org*): Nonprofit, offers a low-cost ($5) Five Wishes healthcare directive on its Website.
- American Bar Association (*www.abanet.org*): Check out its "Public Resources" or "Find Legal Help" links for more information.
- Covenant Consumer Resource Center (*www.covenantresource.com*): A consumer-oriented Website from Matt Rettick and his Covenant Reliance Producers team dedicated to helping pre-retirees and retirees access the necessary information to safeguard their estates and become financially fit for life; check out the free booklets available on a variety of topics.
- Financial Planning Association (*www.fpanet.org*): Financial industry organization, has helpful consumer information on a variety of topics.
- National Hospice and Palliative Care Organization (*www.nhpco.org*): Includes solid information on important end-of-life directives and other issues.

PART II

Physical Fitness

for a Lifetime

Chapter 3

Step 1: Eat Right—

Long-Term Insurance

for Your Body

Physical fitness is more than just exercise and proper nutrition. It's a lifestyle, attitude, and mental commitment as well. Whatever your age, you don't have to be a "usta" person, someone who always says, "I *used to* be able to dance," "I *used to* go swimming or play tennis every day," or "Things *used to* be better in the old days."

We're going to give you a simple program to help you enjoy life more and be the happier for it. Make no mistake: This isn't a "30 days to fitness or your money back" program. This is a new approach to your lifestyle that can change your life, and maybe even your lifespan.

Fitness is about today and tomorrow, and creating a life and lifestyle for the future. You're not going to starve yourself with mini-portions or rob your taste buds of the enjoyment of food. Just the opposite. You can have your cake and eat it too, if it's the right kind of cake in the proper amount. Just don't lose sight of the fact that what you put into your mouth today is walking and talking tomorrow, and has a great deal to do with how you look and feel.

Remember the little experiment in Chapter 1 in which you bent your finger back until it hurt, and then imagined what it would be like to make a financial decision while in pain? Enjoying life without worries and making the most of every day starts with good health so that you don't experience discomfort or pain in any of your activities.

Eating Right

One of the most important aspects of a physical fitness program is good nutrition. Fad diets come and go, and return yet again. But the basis for physical fitness remains constant: eating right.

Eat right and you can't go wrong.

—Jack LaLanne

My wife, Elaine, and I—along with tens of thousands of others we've helped throughout these seven decades-plus of fitness—are living proof that a healthy diet is the backbone of any fitness regimen.

When I first met Elaine, 27 at the time, she was a junk-food junkie, a cigarette smoker, and an addict hooked on chocolate doughnuts and jelly danishes. She paid little attention to my warnings that tomorrow she'd be wearing the foods she ate today. Until one day, she noticed that certain body parts were sagging. Not long after that, she realized tobacco was sapping her energy. So Elaine woke up and decided to take charge of her health. She joined my fitness class, quit smoking, broiled the foods she used to fry, and cut white sugar and flour products from her diet. In one month she reproportioned her body. Her skin became smoother and tighter. Even her vision became more acute, because smoking had been constricting the blood vessels in her eyes. Elaine had become a convert.

We eventually married and became a team that spread the philosophy of exercise and proper nutrition as essentials for life. Today, at age 81, Elaine still works with me to do that.

Art, 53, became a convert to good nutrition too, but for different reasons. He'd been overweight most of his life. In fact, his struggle with his weight started when he was in high school and "bulking up" for the school football team. Unfortunately, he didn't build muscle the right way, with weights and training, but simply piled on the pounds with french fries, steak, chips, and chocolate. By the time he hit middle age, Art had added wine and beer to the mix and suffered from gout as well as high blood pressure. His mother's death was his wake-up call. That's when he truly took stock of his physical health and decided to make some changes before it was too late. He traded in the wine for water, the french fries for fresh fruits and vegetables, and chips for whole grain, no-fat crackers. He dropped 45 pounds and, because he changed his eating habits, is maintaining his new weight. He no longer suffers from high blood pressure or gout and has energy galore to keep up with his young children. He likes himself better too. Just ask him.

Tips for Top Foods

- *Select and serve raw: Ideally, fruits and vegetables should always be as fresh as possible; choose bright, fresh colors (carrots with deep golden hues, celery that is green, root vegetables such as turnips and beets with good green tops); with fruit, pay attention to eye appeal, general appearance, firmness, and ripeness.*

- *Choose whole grains: Opt for brown, unpolished rice instead of white rice; whole wheat or whole rye instead of white flour; brown sugar over white sugar; or opt for honey as a sweetener instead.*

- *Avoid stale foods: Keep food refrigerated, and don't stock up on perishable foods; avoid long storage of leftovers because time, heat, and exposure to air destroy vitamins.*

- **Undercook rather than overcook meals:** *Overcooking can ruin foods' nutritional value, so undercook nearly all your vegetables to preserve vitamin content.*

- **Broil or roast meats:** *Forget frying, because it means adding oil or fat to the process, and that adds calories. On the other hand, with broiling or grilling, the fat drips away, reducing the fat and calorie intake initially associated with the food, as reports nutritionist Gale Rudolph, PhD, CNS.*

- **Use as little water as possible to cook foods:** *If you cook with water, use only the minimum amount needed to create a little steam in order to preserve vitamin content.*

- **Use quality vegetable oils in limited quantities:** *To help limit your intake of animal fats, use only quality vegetable oils such as olive, canola, soy, or peanut oil.*

- **Season only lightly:** *If food is prepared properly and the taste is not cooked out of it, only mild seasoning is sufficient; use seasonings such as garlic powder and vegetable salts.*

You too can step away from the throngs who overeat and overindulge. Eating properly isn't that difficult, especially if you consider the consequences of eating poorly. Remember what happens if you put water in the gas tank of your car? The machine won't run. The same concept applies to the human machine, your body. If you put the wrong fuels into it, the fuel lines—your blood vessels—will clog, and the body won't run. Another analogy: You wouldn't wake up your dog in the morning and give him a cup of coffee, a cigarette, and a donut. That would kill the dog!

Make the personal commitment today to make a difference for yourself and your loved ones.

You are what you eat!

—Jack LaLanne

The Dieter Profile

Can you identify with any of these various types of "dieters?" Note: If you take in more calories than you burn up, you won't lose weight. It's that simple.

- The **Picker, Taster, or Snacker:** Gloria couldn't understand why she gained weight. "Oh, I hardly eat anything all day, and still gain," she complained. Then one day her niece came to visit and pointed out how many times Gloria grabbed a "quick" snack during the day. The Picker picks all day, and each pick has calories. The Glorias of the world are like the newspaper business: Years ago newspapers sold for only 2 cents each, but that created empires. The Picker also starts small, but builds a big corporation (usually in front) before he or she realizes it.

- The **One-Mealer:** Alan ate just one meal a day in the evening, and still gained weight. Findings show that many people who do not eat all day long over-eat at the evening meal, and without realizing it, take in more calories than if they ate three regular meals. They don't burn up all those calories, and the spread takes over.

- **Hidden-Calories Dieter:** Alissa has good intentions! She drinks coffee with no cream, but loads it with sugar; eats a cottage cheese salad for lunch, but tops it off with pie a la mode; broils a lean steak, but stuffs the 75-calorie baked potato with butter and sour cream. You get the picture.

- The **Over-indulger:** George carefully selects only healthy foods, yet he always eats too much at one sitting. One apple a day is good, so why eat 10 of them?

Forget the "Diet"

Our bodies truly are remarkable. Our cells have the ability to replace themselves every 90 days, so it makes sense that what you put in your mouth today will show itself later. It's like planting a garden. What you sow today, you'll reap tomorrow.

Moderation is an essential step to a physically fit way of life. We're not talking about a "diet" like those in-and-out fads we all hear about. As Art learned and profited from, this is a way of life that's neither temporary nor unnatural. It's a new way of thinking about your life and your body.

Let's analyze the word *diet*. What does it mean to you? Is it what you eat every day? Or does it mean hunger, calories, a temporary state, or regimented eating? The first thought that comes into my mind when I hear the word *diet* is *temporary*. Most people who go on a diet end up going off and on and off and on. They lose weight, gain weight, lose weight, and gain weight. It's a vicious cycle that accomplishes little and isn't particularly healthy either.

Our bodies are the houses we live in, and the choices we make help shape those houses. Our bodies house our minds, souls, bones, muscles, and internal organs—all of which allow our bodies to function. The choices we make determine how well our bodies function; each one of us is, in a way, the architect who shapes or designs his or her own body.

It's easy to compare the house that is our body with an actual home. If a house is neglected and poorly maintained, throughout the years it deteriorates and ceases to function properly. The plumbing breaks down, the foundation starts to collapse, the central heating system goes haywire, and the exterior needs to be repainted. In other words, the house is a wreck, and looks old and dilapidated.

The same is true of the human house. If routine maintenance is neglected, the foundation—your 206 bones and 648 muscles—may start to collapse. The internal plumbing won't work regularly, and the central heating system—your body's ability to withstand hot and cold—may not operate properly. The exterior of your human house becomes old and tired-looking too. The texture of your skin loses its elasticity and youthful appearance. Your hair and eyes lose their luster. In other words, if you don't take care of yourself, you'll deteriorate and fall into disrepair, just like an actual building.

The Details of Rebuilding

A damaged building isn't rebuilt without first having a plan. It's the same with rebuilding your body. Lay out and then write down a plan. Decide what you will eat and when, and then keep a record of it all. Not only will writing down your plan reinforce your commitment, but it will also show you concrete and achievable goals. Those nutritional achievements, in turn, (as with financial achievements) will reinforce your positive approach to this new way of life. Let's take a closer look at the elements of your plan.

Fruits and vegetables. Your plan should include a sensible diet with plenty of fresh fruits and vegetables to keep the internal plumbing system (bowels, bladder, arteries, veins, and more) working properly. Leading health authorities recommend that you eat a least five to 10 servings of fruits and vegetables every day, along with a variety of other foods. Include fruits and vegetables high in vitamins A and C (see the vitamin list later in this chapter), such as bananas, avocados, carrots, cabbage, celery, bell peppers, cucumbers, zucchini, apples, oranges, grapefruits, pineapples, grapes, and berries.

One good way to get plenty of raw vegetables—I use up to 10 different kinds at once—is to either chop them finely in a salad or juice them for a healthful drink. If you opt for the salad, don't pile on the dressing, but instead dip your fork into a small dish of dressing beside your plate before each bite. An alternative that cuts down on the amount of dressing, and, in turn, the fat you consume, is to sprinkle a small amount of dressing in a plastic bag, add your salad to the bag, shake, and then serve.

Salt. Use it sparingly, and taste your food first. Remember, salt is an acquired taste. Give yourself a few weeks of little or no salt before you decide if you must have it. If so, use a salt substitute available from your grocer or local health-food stores.

Fat. The body needs a certain amount of fat, but Americans go overboard. No more than 30 percent of your daily food intake should consist of fat. It's really best at 20 to 25 percent. The subject of oils and fats and cholesterol can be confusing, because some people tend to equate oils, fats, and cholesterol.

Following is a list of the three kinds of fat and what they will do for you.

- **Polyunsaturates:** This is a harmless group, and can even have beneficial side effects such as possibly lowering a person's cholesterol level. These oils include safflower oil, soybean oil, corn oil, cottonseed oil, sesame oil, sunflower oils, and most margarines.

- **Monounsaturates:** Another "safe" fat, these include olive oil, canola (rape-seed) oil, and peanut oils.

- **Saturates**: These are troublesome, and include coconut oil, palm kernel and palm oils, and hydrogenated oils. Beyond vegetable oils, wholemilk dairy products, butter, lard, and other animal products also are included in this group.

Vitamins and Antioxidants. Taking vitamin and mineral supplements is an insurance policy for your diet. Even if you eat healthy foods in their natural state, you can't be sure how fresh they are or what their vitamin content is. So, just as we insure our cars, houses, and lives, we ensure our health with vitamin supplements.

Vitamins can be fat soluble, such as A, D, E, and K, or water soluble, such as B and C.

Vitamin Facts

- **Vitamin A:** *Important oil-soluble vitamin that can be obtained from beta carotene; an antioxidant that helps prevent cancer, lowers the risk of heart disease, and aids in eye and skin disorders.* **Sources:** *Yellow and green vegetables such as carrots, sweet potatoes, collards, winter squash, spinach, kale, and broccoli; and fruits, including cantaloupe and apricots.*

- **Vitamin Bs:** *A series of vitamins that affect the nervous system, mental behavior, and more. They're not stored in the body, so it's important to get all the B vitamins daily. Plus, if one is missing it creates a break in the chain so that it no longer works. Following are just some of the important B vitamins:*

  - **Vitamin B 1 (Thiamin):** *Vital in many body functions; helps release energy from food and metabolizes carbohydrates; helps heart and nervous system to function properly.* **Sources:** *Whole-grain products, most vegetables, potatoes, beans, liver, brewer's yeast, and lean meats.*

  - **Vitamin B 2 (Riboflavin):** *Promotes tissue repair, and healthy skin, hair, and nails.* **Sources:** *Eggs, milk, fish, lean meats, poultry, leafy green vegetables, liver, and yeast.*

  - **Vitamin B 3 (Niacin):** *Helps maintain healthy skin, increases circulation, helps in the absorption* of proteins and carbohydrates, contributes to healthy nervous system. **Sources:** Lean meat, fish, poultry, eggs, beans, seeds, whole grains, liver, and brewer's yeast.

- *Vitamin B 5 (Pantothenic Acid):* Helps develop central nervous system, cell and energy builder, metabolizes carbohydrates and fatty acids. **Sources:** Wheat germ, whole wheat, bran, chicken, nuts, green vegetables, kidney, liver, and brewer's yeast.

- *Vitamin B 6 (Pyridoxine):* Needed for healthy teeth and gums, blood vessels, nervous system, and red blood cells. **Sources:** Whole grains, meat, most vegetables, sunflower seeds, beans, wheat germ, liver, and brewer's yeast.

- *Vitamin B 12 (Cobalamin):* Essential for proper development of red blood cells, helps proper function of nervous system, increases energy. **Sources:** liver, kidney, heart, eggs, milk, and milk products. Because research has shown that older people absorb less B12 from their foods, the government recommends they take a B12 supplement. It's good insurance that you're getting enough of this essential vitamin.

- *Vitamin C (Ascorbic Acid):* Important antioxidant that helps reduce the risk of cancer; essential for sound bones and teeth, tissue metabolism and wound healing; builds up immune system and fights infection. **Sources:** Citrus fruits, and green vegetables such as sweet peppers, chard, cabbage, tomatoes, and potatoes.

- *Vitamin D:* Known as the sunshine vitamin, it's essential for calcium and phosphorus metabolism *for strong bones and teeth.* **Sources:** *Sunshine, fish liver oil, sardines, salmon, tuna, and dairy products.*

- **Vitamin E:** *Active antioxidant defends against free radicals, helps maintain heart and skeletal muscles, cuts risk of heart disease, and is believed to help slow the aging process.* **Sources:** *wheat germ, wheat germ oil, vegetable oils, nuts, leafy greens, and whole grain cereals.*

- **Vitamin K:** *Needed for normal blood clotting.* **Sources:** *Green leafy vegetables.*

When trying to find the best vitamin supplement, consider visiting your local health-food store. They generally have the best selection as well as the latest information on all vitamins. Another great vitamin resource is *Earl Mindell's New Vitamin Bible: 25th Anniversary Edition*, by Earl Mindell and Hester Mundis (Warner Books, 2004). It's available at most bookstores, online at Amazon.com, or directly from Mindell's Website (*www.earlmindell.com*).

Minerals. Everyone talks about vitamins, but minerals are equally important to our general health, growth, and body maintenance. Our bodies don't manufacture minerals, so we must acquire them from the environment. Keep in mind that trace elements such as zinc and chromium are reduced when grains are refined. Also, if the soil a food is grown in is depleted in a particular mineral, the food grown will be deficient too.

Be careful when taking minerals. Ingesting large amounts of some minerals can lead to deficiencies in others, as well as other problems. Sodium (as in common salt) and potassium regulate the body's water balance. Too much sodium depletes potassium and can throw off the balance. This can result in high blood pressure and water retention.

For purposes of nutrition, minerals are lumped together either as major minerals, of which the body needs sizable amounts, or trace elements, of which the body requires only small amounts. Major minerals include calcium, magnesium, phosphorus, potassium, and sodium. Trace minerals include chromium, iron, iodine, sulfur, zinc, selenium, manganese, copper, cobalt, fluorine, and molybdenum.

Fiber. Don't overlook getting enough fiber either. Eat it regularly to help with elimination. That's especially true for older adults.

Protein. This is "the keystone of human nutrition," according to Lester M. Morrison, MD, a California cardiologist who, in the early 1950s, was a pioneer advocate of low-cholesterol, low-fat diets for heart health. (To prove his point, he placed 50 of his seriously ill heart patients on a diet that imitated the low-cholesterol, low-fat food rations characteristic of Europeans in World War II. Another 50 of his equally ill patients continued on their typical high-fat American diet. Of course, the low-fat, low-cholesterol group prevailed!)

In other words, protein is essential to life. Normal adults and growing children require 1 gram of protein for every 2.2 pounds (equal to1 kilogram) of body weight. That means the average man or woman who weighs 125 to 175 pounds needs 60 to 80 grams of protein daily for normal nutrition. And because the body doesn't store protein for future needs, we must continually replenish supplies.

The protein picture can get confusing, but basically, protein is made up of a chain of amino acids that in turn are divided into two groups: essential, those provided in your food; and nonessential, those manufactured by the body. Also, there are two types of proteins: complete and incomplete. Complete proteins (meats, seafood, poultry, eggs, milk, and cheese) contain all the essential amino acids to support new tissue growth, whereas the incomplete proteins (nuts, seeds, peas, grains, and beans) are in insufficient amounts and need essential amino acids to make them complete.

Lentils and rice, for example, each are incomplete proteins, but when eaten together become complete, because one has what the other is lacking. Adding an egg white to either also would make a complete protein. Just remember to complement your protein sources. (Note: Making an incomplete protein complete doesn't necessarily require an animal protein.)

Starch. Here's a trick question: Starch is a term describing white foods that make you fat because they're nothing but empty calories, true or false?

If you answered "true," then you have fallen prey to one of the most pervasive nutritional myths circulating today. Starchy foods, in fact, are generally low in fat or fat-free, and low in sodium (except processed foods). Many starchy foods also are high in essential vitamins and minerals. The potato is a good example of a nutritious starch. Eat it with the skin on to get important dietary fiber, vitamin C, and potassium.

Starch is a form of complex carbohydrate found in a variety of foods of all different colors. Foods high in starch include grains, legumes, and some other vegetables. That encompasses breads, cereals, pasta, rice, potatoes, peas, corn, and beans. Brown rice and whole grains also provide protein, potassium, and phosphorus.

A Word on Calories

Calories, a measure of the amount of energy stored in a food, are used by the body to convert that food to energy. If we consume more calories a day than we burn, the excess calories become stored as fat (one pound of excess weight equals about 3,500 calories). I don't count calories, but calories do count, and taking in more than you use will pile on the pounds.

Instead of fretting about the exact calorie count of everything you ingest, lump foods into groups of high calories or low calories. First group your foods as vegetables, fruits, whole gains, dairy products, meats, poultry, and fish. Then learn what foods are high and low calorie in each category.

Whenever you start to take a bite of a high-calorie food, ask yourself, "What is this doing for me? Will it make me slim and trim, or will it just add more pounds to my body?"

The number of calories you as an individual need each day depends on you, the amount of activity in your life, and other factors. The average person who gets moderate activity needs an estimated 15 calories per pound of body weight per day. If your normal body weight is 160 pounds, for example, you might need approximately 2,400 calories a day. If you are very active and work hard, you might need an additional 500 to 1,000 calories. Conversely, if you're particularly sedentary you might be better off with 300 to 400 fewer calories.

> *Don't exceed the feed limit!*
>
> —*Jack LaLanne*

Beyond strictly the numbers, the kinds of calories make a difference too. You can lose weight on 1,000 calories a day of either candy bars or nutritional foods. But the candy, which is made up of empty calories, will leave you with hunger pangs and mood swings from its sugar high.

Age is a factor too, when it comes to calorie intake. Generally, the older you are, the fewer calories your body requires. That's because your metabolism slows and your physical activities aren't as vigorous as when you were younger. Are you getting the message? It's that "get up and get going" line again!

Family History

Heart disease remains the number-one killer in North America. Some of the risk factors for heart disease—such as heredity—are beyond our control. But others aren't. By emphasizing fresh produce and avoiding fatty snacks and excessive red meat, you'll automatically reduce cholesterol levels that can affect your heart health. Remember, cholesterol comes from animals and animal products, including milk.

It's not in fruits or vegetables. It's not in popcorn, for example, unless it's buttered!

If you have a family history of heart disease, then you especially should watch your fats and probably your cholesterol intake. Otherwise, if you exercise at least 20 minutes a day, four to five days a week, you'll most likely keep your LDL, or "bad" cholesterol levels, down, and the HDL, or good cholesterol levels, raised. Take the path to long life and health by making wise choices with everyday fitness and nutritious food.

Visible Results

Change doesn't happen overnight, but chances are you'll feel more energetic pretty quickly. You should begin to see and feel small improvements in your body within the first week of exercising and eating right. A good example is my friend Sam, who started out at 300 pounds. He began walking just one mile a day, stopped using cream and sugar in his coffee, and cut out pizza, cheeseburgers, and french fries, substituting them with fresh salads, fruits, and a juicing regimen. He lost 9 pounds the first week! Six weeks later, he was walking five miles a day and had dropped 30 pounds. Not only did he lose the pounds, but also his mental outlook changed with his newfound energy.

Gradually, as your body gets ample nutrients, your skin will regain a more youthful glow, your eyes will become more alert, your hair more lustrous, and your nails stronger. This is not a pipedream. It's the reality of what good nutrition can and does do for all of us.

My dad committed suicide with his knife and fork!

—*Jack LaLanne*

Edna could not control her appetite. She dieted constantly, but always found herself cheating. Her eating was so out of control that she decided to have part of her stomach removed so that she could no longer consume so much food. After the operation, her weight dropped dramatically and she looked fantastic. Sadly though, this change lasted only a short time before she discovered she could drink milkshakes and slather her food with high-cholesterol sauces. So even though her portions were small, she replaced the calories she used to eat with those in liquid form. Her weight ballooned, and within a short period of time she was right back where she started. That's why a regimen of exercise and proper nutrition is so very important.

Eating Patterns and Obesity

As a solution to the weight issue, some people advocate eating five or more smaller meals as opposed to three main meals every day. Not enough evidence exists yet to determine if that's a valid approach. But keep in mind that if the overall quantity of food is the same, whether consumed in three main meals or five or six smaller, regular meals or snacks, the effect should be the same.

Exceptions, of course, exist. Diabetics, for example, find that eating small, regular meals is more beneficial than eating three main meals. Many people also resist changing their eating habits, so even if you don't change the frequency of *your* meals, dietary changes such as reducing the intake of high-fat snacks can be beneficial.

Let's also consider the eating patterns of people in various countries and how that might or might not contribute to obesity. The French generally eat three discrete meals with little or no snacking. The prevalence of obesity in their country is low compared with countries such as the United States and Australia, where snacking on high-fat foods is more common.

Going Natural

The word *natural* is overused and misused these days, as is the term *organic*. The federal government has even gotten involved in defining the latter because of misleading advertising. But let's simplify it all: Figure it's best to eat natural foods in their natural state to the greatest extent possible. Peel a banana, cut a ripe pineapple, crunch a raw zucchini, or savor a raw mushroom, for example, and you're getting the full benefit of a food's nutritional value.

Eat Fresh

Did you know:

- *Sodium levels in canned food can be as much as four times higher than their fresh or even frozen counterpart?*

- *The physical bulk created by eating fresh produce can help "fill you up" with less food? Eating a big bowl of fresh spinach will fill you up more than a few bites of the cooked variety.*

- *The air volume whipped into a smoothie that you drink goes a lot further toward filling you up than the same amount of juice from a can?*

Source: Nutritionist Gale Rudolph, PhD, CNS

Healthy Choices

Breakfast:

- **Healthy version:** *Three-egg-white omelet with fresh tomatoes, onion, bell pepper, and mushrooms, whole wheat toast, and a glass of fresh juice.*

- **Unhealthy version:** *Bacon, eggs with yolk, hash browns, white-bread toast, and coffee with cream and sugar.*

Lunch:

- **Healthy version:** *Toasted turkey sandwich on whole wheat bread with lettuce and tomato, four pieces of fresh fruit or a fresh fruit cup, and fresh fruit juice or plain water.*

- **Unhealthy version:** *Double cheeseburger, french fries, and a bottle of pop or a milkshake.*

Dinner:

- **Healthy version:** *Broiled fresh fish; brown rice cooked with celery, onions, and bell pepper; a salad of five to 10 raw vegetables; and a dessert of smashed bananas and honey.*

- **Unhealthy version:** *Macaroni and cheese, canned spinach, white bread and butter, and pie a la mode for dessert.*

Going natural isn't particularly difficult today either. You can find organic and natural food stores in virtually any metropolitan area. But it wasn't always that easy. It used to be that people scoffed at eating raw mushrooms, laughed at carrot juice, and rejected nutrition the LaLanne way. Now cold juice bars are hot, as is the subject of nutrition. In the 1930s, people had no clue that eating foods in their natural state would help them live longer. White flour, sugar, and lard were the norm. Obesity was accepted. To eat natural meant we had to make or grow food ourselves.

We couldn't just head down the street to the juice bar in the mall or to the health-food store to pick up a ready-made natural salad.

Back then, and today, a healthy salad consists of five to 10 raw vegetables, such as avocados, carrots, cabbage, celery, bell peppers, cucumbers, tomatoes, and zucchini. Don't forget to eat three or four pieces of fresh fruits, either, such as apples, oranges, grapefruits, pineapple, grapes, bananas, and cherries.

A Note of Caution: Just because a label says *natural* doesn't mean a food is good for you. Read the details on the labels. Also steer clear of many foods that are dead, or lacking in nutritional value. Canned and processed foods are good examples of those.

Pay attention to the "sell by" or related date that appears on foods as well as the complete nutritional information list on labels, such as calories per serving, calories from fat, total fat and saturated fat, cholesterol, sodium carbohydrate, and protein. (Check out the U.S. Department of Agriculture's Food Safety and Inspection Service Website for more on labeling: *www.fsis.usda.gov*.)

Remember, we eat for health, for fitness, for youth, for beauty, and for personal magnetism. That's no joke!

Check out MyPyramid (www.mypyramid.gov) *from the U.S. Department of Agriculture, an interactive tool to help all of us get our nutrition on track.*

Real Stories

Changing your eating habits can be surprisingly simple once you've made the commitment to better nutrition. All it takes, as Mary discovered, is a little inspiration to get started. "I used to eat a lot of junk food, but just changed a few bad habits for good ones so that I really don't feel like I'm depriving myself at all," she says. Instead of frying foods in a lot of oil, she opts to sauté them in a tiny amount of olive oil or even a little vegetable or chicken broth. Instead of whole milk, she uses skim, and instead of gooey deserts, she chooses a smashed banana with honey and lemon juice. "It's become so easy to substitute the good for the bad, and fun too," she says.

Tasty, Healthy-Minded Tips

- *Sweetener for cereal:* Pour apple juice over cereal.

- *Smashed bananas:* Mash bananas with a fork and add coconut and strawberries.

- *Potatoes LaLanne:* Slice potatoes, season, and place under the broiler.

- *Salt substitute:* Try garlic or onion powder.

- *Salt substitute II:* Try herbs, pepper, and lemon juice.

- *Breakfast alternative:* 1 pint fresh juice, 1 banana, 30 to 40 grams protein powder; liquefy in power blender and serve immediately.

- *Potato skins:* Brush a potato skin with a little oil, season with garlic, and then broil until crisp.

- *Omelet option:* Substitute egg whites for whole eggs, and fill with fresh vegetables.

- *Butter alternative:* Try olive or canola oil sparingly and add chopped garlic.

- *Low-calorie bread:* Take the inside out of the bread and toast the crust crisp.

The Other Half of the Equation

Eat right and you stand a better chance of living a long, healthy life—with one caveat. You'll just get by unless you combine proper nutrition with the other half of the physical fitness equation: exercise. So get ready to get up and go.

> *When you take up a fitness lifestyle, the only thing you stand to lose is what you didn't want anyway!*
>
> —Jack LaLanne

Roadmap to Success

Changing your approach to what and how much you eat doesn't have to be boring, and it's as easy as exchanging a bad habit for a good one. It takes commitment, conviction, and the right guidance.

No matter your age, keep in mind:

- Our bodies are like houses; if we don't take care of them and maintain them properly, they'll become dilapidated and fall apart.
- If you take in more calories than you burn up, you won't lose weight.
- Eat food in as natural a state as possible, as opposed to processed foods.
- Starchy foods are generally low in fat and sodium, and loaded with essential vitamins and minerals. It's what you add to them that piles on the calories!

More Resources

- American Dietetic Association (*www.eatright.org*): From the nation's largest organization of food and nutrition specialists; click on "Food and Nutrition" for valuable reading and links to additional information sources.

- Centers for Disease Control and Prevention (*www.cdc.gov*): From the U.S. Department of Health and Human Services, includes a wealth of information on health, aging, and medical issues.

- Jack LaLanne (*www.jacklalanne.com*): LaLanne's philosophy of health and fitness, exercise tips, recipes, and more; includes section for sale of LaLanne's books, tapes, DVDs, juicers, and other items.

- MyPyramid.gov (*www.mypyramid.gov*): From the U.S. Department of Agriculture, helps individuals determine the types and amounts of food to fit their needs; includes interactive tools as well as government guidelines for nutrition and tips for fitness.

- Fifty Plus Lifelong Fitness (*www.50plus.org*): Nonprofit that promotes an active lifestyle for older people; click on Resources for links to all types of organizations and information sources.

- Prevention Magazine (*www.prevention.com*): Every month the magazine brings you up-to-date health information that can help you better achieve a healthy lifestyle.

- Shape Up America (*www.shapeup.org*): A nonprofit with the purpose of educating the public about the importance of achieving and maintaining a healthy body weight through increased physical activity and healthy eating; includes interactive tools and information on weight loss.

Chapter 4

Step 2: Exercise for Life—

Building Your Body's

Bank Account

> *Being fit does not cure any diseases. It merely works to prevent them.*
>
> —*Jack LaLanne*

Nutrition goes hand in hand with exercise. You can eat perfectly, but without exercise you'll lose muscle tone. On the other hand, if you exercise vigorously but your diet is lacking, you'll look good physically, but could be a mess internally. Many people look to fad diets for help. Those diets result in weight loss, but without exercise, the dieter often ends up with rolls of flab.

No matter your age, it's not too late to get back in shape. Dividends include not only looking and feeling better, but big potential savings on medical bills and long-term care costs too. When you're sedentary, your blood flow is sluggish and you feel lethargic. As exercise accelerates your blood flow, you become more alert, and you'll be able to power your way through life. Pre-retirement or retirement is the perfect time to make a contract with your body for long-term self-improvement. After all, you want to enjoy your retirement rather than struggle through it. Once the contract is signed, it's your commitment to a better life.

The feeling of being "over the hill" affects your life only if you allow it to. Age, after all, is just a number. If you're sick and tired of being sick and tired, make the change to physical fitness. Make that contract with yourself. Aging needn't be a time of great deterioration if you invest a little effort in proper nutrition and taking better care of your body. Doing so will revitalize your life.

A Contract With Yourself to Achieve Fitness

1. *This agreement, dated _____ is among _____ [your name], The Mind, and The Body, henceforth for the purposes of this Agreement as witnessed in spirit by Jack LaLanne, Morro Bay, California.*

2. *The purpose of this Agreement is to get in better shape and improve overall vitality, mental outlook, and overall well-being. Party No. 1, The Mind, grants Party No. 2, The Body, the sole and exclusive right to adapt and change The Body and to increase overall strength and stamina.*

3. *It is understood that Jack LaLanne will provide guidance to help The Mind and The Body fulfill this ambition through the tips and goals set forth in this book.*

4. *The underweight will strive to follow the suggestions to normalize their weight, and the overweight will do their best to lose those extra pounds.*

5. *Both parties understand that maintaining a good quality of life requires using The Body's ability to strengthen itself or risk losing itself.*

6. *Further, the term of this agreement is for life.*

7. *The territory is worldwide.*

8. *Compensation: Both parties understand that the compensation for the effort is looking better, feeling better, and the possibility of a longer, more fulfilling life.*

Signed this day:

_____   *Jack LaLanne*

Representing The Mind and The Body   Jack LaLanne in spirit

Your Insurance

We all like to feel, act, and look younger. The cosmetic industry takes in literally billions of dollars annually on just that premise. One easy way to ensure youthful results is to get in good physical shape. All it takes is attention to nutrition and as little as 12 to 18 minutes of exercise a day. You can't get that assurance from a face cream at the cosmetics counter.

Realistically, an 80-year-old woman who exercises will never look like a 19-year-old, but she can be the most youthful 80-year-old you've even seen! Even if it doesn't show as much on the outside, physical fitness nets results on the inside. When you're fit, it's much easier to perform those tasks and achieve those goals that perhaps have been just beyond reach. Remember, inactivity is the essence of decay.

Exercise helps us better assimilate our food and get more nutrition from fewer calories. It also helps regulate our appetite, promote regularity, metabolize and utilize vitamins and minerals, and sleep better along the way, as well as fighting degenerative diseases, arteriosclerosis, and high blood pressure.

Lack of Fitness Is Revealing

Let's analyze what happens to someone who's not fit:
- Muscles weaken, soften, lose efficiency
- Waistline bulges

- Behind droops or sags
- Posture droops
- Circulation slows
- Faulty elimination sets in
- Sleeplessness occurs
- Ambition decreases
- Face looks tired
- Zest for life diminishes
- Memory wanes

Do you identify with any of these? If so, perhaps it's time to examine your own physical fitness. (We'll show you specific exercises tailored to combat these woes later in this chapter.)

As a child I broke my arm trying to crank our old Model T Ford. (Back then cars didn't have automatic starters and relied on elbow grease instead.) My arm ended up in a cast for months. When the cast came off, the arm was scrawny and shriveled to the point that I could hardly move it. Inactivity had eaten away the arm's muscle tone and elasticity. The same kind, if not degree, of atrophy can afflict your body without exercise. Do you doubt that? In more than 70 years as a physical culturist and fitness teacher I've seen literally thousands of people who are living proof!

Forget those excuses too. Even if you have $10 million in the bank, a family, and friends, how can you truly enjoy your good fortune if you're not physically and comfortably fit?

Lack of time is the biggest excuse for not exercising. "Look Jack, I know I should exercise. I'd really like to be in better shape and lose weight. But I work, I go to school, I have kids and a family and pets to take care of, I'm too busy. And besides that, I just don't have the time."

Well, now is the time to reconsider that excuse, because it doesn't take as much time as you think to achieve better physical fitness.

Dare to Dream

Our minds control everything. If you want to improve yourself, you must take charge and send a message to your body's 70-billion-plus cells that they will be better off with proper exercise and better nutrition. If you send negative signals to your body, you'll get negative results. Instead, concentrate on sending positive signals to get positive results. We all should set goals, and then dream about them.

When I decided to get fit, I had a very definite idea of how I wanted to look and feel. Specifically, my goal was a body similar to that of a famous Indian fitness expert at the time, K.V. Iyer. I posted his body measurements and pictures around my room and in my schoolbooks. Every week I would weigh myself, take my measurements, and dream about my new body. It was a visual, physical, emotional, and mental experience. When I achieved my goal—his measurements—I set new goals, and continued to dream and fantasize about my projected improvements. I painted a picture in my mind of what I wanted to be. If I hadn't dared to dream, I would never have accomplished my goals.

We all have dreams and goals. Not everyone, however, follows through on them. With the right mindset and attitude, you *can* be among those who do. If you have a weight problem, you must count calories. You must think positively. Too often, negative thoughts creep in and spoil the dream. Weight loss is foiled by thoughts such as:

- "I'm too old."
- "I can't lose weight."
- "I hate to exercise."
- "I can't afford it."
- "I'm not smart enough."
- "My metabolism doesn't work anymore."

Why not look on the positive side of the issue instead? Every day in every way tell yourself that you're getting better and better, that you're the luckiest person alive, and that you can and will do this. Feed your mind the seeds of positive thinking, and dare to dream.

After three children and 20 years as a secretary behind a desk—not to mention years of between-meal snacking and overindulging—Ann, 45, was overweight and out of shape. When the family hit the ski slopes, she sat in the lodge. When they went to the beach, she stayed home, embarrassed to be seen in a bathing suit. Exasperated with her 100-plus extra pounds and all the failed fad diets she'd tried through the years, she finally decided to attempt something different. She'd heard about the LaLanne natural way of healthy eating combined with exercise, and decided to make a commitment to it.

> *It takes six to seven weeks from the time you begin a fitness program until you become reasonably fit. But don't get discouraged. You will see results along the way. Considering the years of unfitness leading up to your new lifestyle, that seems like a pretty good deal.*
>
> —*Jack LaLanne*

Ann couldn't believe how quickly the pounds melted away just by cutting out between-meal snacks, trading off fat foods for healthy ones, losing the salt, and spending 30 minutes a day with the Magic Five (see pages 97 and 98). "The first few weeks were tough," says Ann. "But then I actually began to look forward to taking my measurements and seeing the changes in my body. I look great and feel 15 years younger!"

After four months of the program, a confident Ann outruns her teenagers on the ski slopes and has once again become a beach fanatic.

Arnie, 62 and a widower, was frail yet overweight, and his children constantly worried about his health. Ever since his wife died several years earlier, he had basically just shut down. At meals he barely ate except for desserts because, he said, food bored him. Once an avid outdoor enthusiast, he now sat around the house and brooded. He wasn't even interested in his own grandchildren. His doctors had ruled out clinical depression and other physical ailments. One night while flipping through the rerun channels, he stumbled on *The Jack LaLanne Show* and stopped. "I was surprised that an old man could do that sort of thing," Arnie says, "And I was intrigued by his approach to food. So I tried it."

Once Arnie started getting the nutrition and physical exercise he needed, he quickly rebounded to his old self. He began feeling better internally and externally, and started to enjoy life again.

Mental Commitment

Remember, fear begets more fear. And fear leads to the "I can't" syndrome. Just as someone says he or she doesn't have the self-control to put away money, many people lament that they can't stick to a good diet or stay on an exercise program. But you *can* become fiscally and physically fit if you truly try. All it takes to get started is commitment. And once you get started, fitness gets easier and easier, until eventually it's a habit.

Virtually everything we do in life is a matter of habit. Habits make us who we are. Why not change your habits to better your life? You *can* do it, and it's not that difficult. When you put aside money regularly, you watch it compound and grow. Similarly, changing to good nutrition and regular exercise compounds your commitment because you start to feel better about yourself, physically and mentally. A change for the better has positive effects on everything you do in life.

Age is mostly immaterial. You can change your body if you make the decision to truly do so. As an added bonus, your exercise regimen can be a special time in your day that promotes clear thinking while building a sense of well-being and increased self-esteem, not to mention burning away unwanted body fat. Don't think for a minute that spending time on yourself in this way is a selfish pursuit. Time spent exercising gives you the energy and clear-headedness to deal effectively with your world and to be the best you can be for the people around you.

> *Anything in life is possible, and you can make it happen.*
>
> *—Jack LaLanne*

Assess Your Assets, Liabilities

If you're seriously ready to change your body, it's time to assess where you stand—what your body's assets and liabilities are. Just as the first step to financial fitness is to take stock of your financial situation—to figure your net worth—so it is with physical fitness. You must figure out where your body is today.

Too many people put too much emphasis on scales and losing weight. But the scale doesn't tell you all the real improvements you're making to your body. So, instead of relying on the scale, get out that tape measure and get in front of a mirror. Most of us want good proportions—the ratio of chest to waist to hips. That's as important to men as it is to women. We all can't be taller or shorter, nor can we put on muscles a la body builders extraordinaire. But we all can improve the bodies we have. The secret to making the most of yourself is taking what you have and putting it where you want it.

Think of yourself as a walking billboard. Does your billboard advertise: "I hate to exercise. I overeat, and I don't care how I look and feel"? If so, it's never too late to change the message to: "I exercise regularly, eat sensibly, and I'm proud of the way I look and feel because I made it happen."

Assessing your body requires honesty. Take off all your clothes and, with tape measure in hand, stand bravely before that full-length mirror with your eyes wide open. What do you see? Don't hold in your stomach, don't tilt your head to get the best profile; see yourself as you are, and then imagine yourself as you want to be. You have now taken the first step toward physical fitness.

Next, take your actual measurements. Don't be afraid of the results either. This is a new beginning, and you can't figure out where you're going if you don't know where you're starting. (See worksheet.)

Your Measurements

WOMEN

Chest

Largest circumference (around bust):

Under bust:

Arms

Extend and measure largest part of upper arm:

Waist

High (just below the rib cage):

Middle (at smallest part):

Low (just above the hip):

Hips

Measure around largest circumference:

Thighs

Largest part, near groin:

Smaller part, above knee:

Calf

Largest part:

Ankle

Measure at smallest part:

Weight

Without clothing, when you get up in the morning:

MEN

Neck:

Chest

Normal (straight across chest):

Chest expanded:

Arms

Upper arm, largest part flexed:

Waist

High:

Middle:

Low:

Hips:

Thighs

Largest part:

Above knee:

Lower Leg

Largest part:

Ankle

At smallest point:

Weight

Without clothing, when you get up in the morning:

After you've taken your measurements, take a picture of yourself. Do that periodically as you get into the program to physical fitness. You'll be amazed at the differences in your body, and your enthusiasm to stay on the program will grow as your body reshapes itself.

Now it's time to take action. If you start with simple steps, it's easier to stay motivated and work toward your fitness goals. Here are five simple exercises to get you started. I call these exercises "The Magic Five," because if you commit to doing these exercises regularly, you'll see "magic" changes in your measurements.

The Magic Five

1. Crunches (in bed or on the floor)

- *Gets the circulation moving*

- *Helps firm up the waistline*

- *Flattens the tummy*

    Lying flat on your back, bend your knees, keeping heels as close to buttocks as possible. With hands either behind your head or across your chest, try to sit up to your knees. Exhale as you sit up, inhale as you lie down. Repeat five times. Rest, and repeat five times.

2. Leg curls (beginners start with one leg at a time)

- *Helps firm out-of-condition muscles*

- *Puts pep in your step and a smile on your face*

    Lie on your back, legs extended, arms extended along sides. Lift knees into chest. At the same time, raise head, tucking chin into chest. Return to start position, repeat five times. Rest, and do five more.

3. Fanny firmer

- *Helps firm the hips and thighs*

    Begin standing. Lean forward, placing hands on edge of bed or chair. Lift right leg back as high as you can without straining. Return to start position and repeat five times on the right leg, then five with the left leg. Rest, and repeat five times on each leg.

4. Running in place (for those who can't run, lift legs as high as possible in walking position)

- Overall body-conditioning exercise

Stand in one place and start running. Lift legs high, knees into body. Swing arms vigorously as if you wanted to punch a hole through the ceiling. Keep shoulders back, head high, and breathe deeply. Run for 30 seconds the first day, and then try to go longer each day.

5. Dynamic stretch

- Muscle-toning exercise

Standing with feet apart, lock hands behind back and extend arms out, trying to touch elbows together. At the same time, keep your head straight by looking at the wall in front of you. Now hold the position and lean forward at the waist. Return to start position and repeat five times. Rest, and do more as able.

The Details

Of course, if you haven't done any exercise for years and have grown creaky and stiff as a result, you'll first need to check with your doctor, and then begin slowly, and do what you can. Your contract for self-improvement is in the form of exercise goals each day. Consider working your upper body one day, your lower body the next, and then resting on the third day.

Some exercise experts advocate exercising only every other day,or every two days, or some such program. But in my 70-plus years of studying physical fitness and the human body, including the longest-running physical fitness series on television—37 years—I've found the best results come from regular and frequent exercise. At minimum, start every day with the Magic Five if it's adaptable to your physical limitations. For optimal results, follow it up later with more exercises, or fitness activities such as bicycling, swimming, walking, or running.

Always start out slowly and do only what's comfortable. When it comes to an exercise program, you just can't pick up where you left off 20 years ago. Remember, your body is a machine. If it's not used, it rusts. You need to work up to things. Make haste slowly.

> *To rest is to rust!*
>
> *—Jack LaLanne*

The first hike I ever took with my wife (we're avid hikers even today) was up the Ledge Trail in Yosemite National Park, California. For those of you who haven't tried it, that trail is one mile almost straight up the side of a mountain. Elaine, age 30 at the time, thought she was in relatively good shape, and started out just fine. But as we headed upward, the signs of "pooped-out-itis" became evident. I ended up carrying her much of the way. But that day she learned a good lesson about getting started on the path to fitness. Make haste slowly—or crawl, walk, and then run. Start out very easily, and then increase the intensity and repetitions as your physical condition improves. Starting out slowly is especially important for older people, because it helps prevent injury as well as the frustration from doing too much too soon that can result in quitting.

Here are a few more things to keep in mind:

- The more you use your body, the better it keeps.
- The best time to exercise is up to you and your schedule; be consistent, and don't exercise for one hour after meals.

- Wear loose-fitting, comfortable clothing.

- If possible, exercise with the windows open to get plenty of fresh air, and never hold your breath. Exhale through your mouth and inhale through your nose.

- Always start with a series of warm-up exercises to get the blood circulating, speed up the action of the heart and lungs, and stretch and limber up the muscles.

- Do your exercises in sets. For example, if you do 10 repetitions of an exercise, repeat it three times, resting between each of the three sets.

- Don't tire yourself out. As your stamina improves after a couple of weeks, rest only as long as you need.

- Train, don't strain.

- Set a goal of doing a little more each day, and concentrate on each exercise. The more slowly you can do an exercise, the more effective it will be.

- As your physical fitness improves, try to go from one exercise to another without resting in between. Change your program every 30 days to avoid monotony.

The Importance of Stretching

Always stretch at the beginning of your workout to condition your muscles and to avoid stiffness and soreness as well as muscle strain. Think about stretching as an energy boost for your body. You can even do special stretches before you get out of bed in the morning.

Whenever and wherever you stretch, you'll feel better for it. Check out our series of stretches on the following pages.

Stretch Away

Try this series of stretches every other day. On your days off, pick any two from the list to supplement your routine:

- **Knee and thigh stretch:** Use your left hand to balance yourself against a wall or a chair; bend your right knee back and grasp your ankle with your right hand; pull up to stretch the thigh muscle. Be sure to maintain good posture. Now switch sides, balancing with the right hand, bending the left knee and holding the ankle with your left hand. Hold for a count of five.

- **Side-to-side stretch:** Spread feet shoulder-width apart; lift your arms over your head, palms facing, fingers touching; now reach for the sky; keeping your feet planted, bend at the waist from side to side. Continue bending side to side until you've completed five reps per side for a total of 10 times.

- **Through-the-legs stretch:** Plant your feet shoulder-width apart; bend forward at the waist, knees bent slightly (that relieves the strain on your lower back); bring your hands through your legs, attempting to touch the floor and wall behind you. Hold for a count of five. Increase the duration as your body adjusts to the activity.

- **Hamstring stretch:** Place feet shoulder-width apart; bend forward at the waist, knees bent slightly; allow hands to drop down in front of feet as though trying to touch the floor; now lift toes off the floor. Hold for a count of two.

- **Knee to chest:** Stand erect with feet shoulder-width apart; place your hands behind your head; bring the right knee up to try to touch the left elbow; alternate. Repeat five times on each leg for a total of 10. Be sure you're bringing the knee up to the elbow, not the elbow down to the knee.

- **Leg lunges to the side**: Stand erect, hands on hips (or on a chair for balance, especially when you first start); lunge to the right with the right leg; step back and lunge to the left with the left leg. Repeat for three counts on each leg for a total of six reps.

- **Windmill stretch**: Stand with feet shoulder-width apart, arms extended outward to the sides; bend over at the waist, knees bent slightly, and try to touch the left hand to the ceiling while grasping the left ankle with the right hand; alternate, reaching the right hand to the ceiling while grasping the right ankle with the left hand. Repeat five times on each side for a total of 10 reps.

- **Rag-doll stretch:** With feet shoulder-width apart, bend at the waist, legs straight; try to keep your back flat and allow your arms to hang loosely; hold for a count of 10 and then shake all over. Make one or two long stretches.

- **Doorway stretch:** Hold on to the framework on both sides of a door; gently try to walk forward as far as possible, stretching your arms; back up and repeat the process five times. Hold each stretch for a count of five.

Benefits From Multitasking

To net faster results from a daily exercise program, try working on some of your problem zones occasionally during the day while you're doing other things, whether sitting at your desk, watching television, standing around the water cooler, in the checkout line, or in the shower. Think of it in the same way that you think of putting money into your savings: The more you put in, the more interest you get back.

A few suggestions:

- Take dynamic breaths for a quick "pick-me-up" and a feeling of well-being.
- Try holding your waist in for five seconds, and then exhale slowly.
- Try a few standing pushups against the wall or counter.
- Contract the buttocks muscles.
- If you're reaching up for something, stretch way up or way out.
- If you're standing around, move up and down on tiptoe to strengthen the calf muscles.
- Other standing-around exercises: Try shoulder shrugs, facial exercises, side bends, ceiling stretches.
- Sitting-around exercises: leg raises, leg cross-overs, push your legs against the floor as hard as you can for 10 seconds; press your elbows in as tightly as you can for 10 seconds; sit up straight and draw your waist in for 10 seconds.

Head-to-Toe Exercises for Your Health

Here's a simple exercise routine to help any age group head to toe. It's also important to change your workouts every three to four weeks so that your muscles don't get used to the same thing. By changing your workout, you are challenging your muscles.

- ***Neck and throat*** *(Up-and-Down Neck Conditioner): Place fingertips on your forehead and apply gentle, constant resistance against your forehead. Lift your head up and look at the ceiling,* *then bring your head down, and try to place your chin on your chest. Pause for a second and then bring your head back up to look at the ceiling. Begin with eight repetitions and work up to 15.*

- **Shoulder shrugs:** *Stand straight, feet shoulder-width apart. Relax your shoulders. Now, bring shoulders up toward your ears, hold for a count of three, then roll your shoulders back toward your back, holding for another count of three, then return to the starting position. Begin with eight repetitions and work up to 15.*

- **Rising to the occasion** *(for back of arms): Sit in an armchair. Place your hands firmly on the arms of the chair, and then lift your body out of the chair by using only your arms. You should feel the back of your arms doing most of the work. Begin with five repetitions and work up to 10.*

- **Arm curls, palms up** *(for front of arms): Using a weight of some kind (books, canned goods, dumbbells, etc.), stand tall, waist in, with your arms extended in front of you, your elbows cocked. Hold your weights with your palms up. Smoothly and slowly lift the weights to your shoulders. Concentrate on the exercise. Return your arms to their original position. Begin with eight repetitions and work up to 15.*

- **Forearm newspaper roll** *(for hands and forearms): Grasp a section of newspaper with both hands. Extend your arms straight out in front of you and then begin to roll up the newspaper. Roll with a great deal of energy and speed. The more resistance you can make the newspaper provide,* *the better. Begin with eight repetitions and work up to 15.*

- **Doorway pushups for chest:** *This is a vertical push-up. Stand in front of a wall, about two feet away from it, with your legs spread to shoulder width. Lean forward against the wall and spread your hands against it. Now, push yourself away from the wall until your arms are straight. Pause a moment and lower yourself back toward the wall. Begin with eight repetitions and work to 15.*

- **Inner thigh resistor:** *Sit on a chair, and place your hands on the insides of the opposite knees. Now, while applying pressure against the knees with the hands, attempt to bring the knees together. Release just enough pressure to allow your knees to part, and then bring them back together, always applying pressure with the hands. Begin with eight repetitions and work up to 15.*

- **Double leg curl to chest:** *Sit on an armless chair, and extend your legs straight out in front of you while grasping the sides of the chair with your hands. Now, bring your knees together to your chest, pause, and lower your feet to the floor. To increase difficulty, try doing the exercise with a book clasped between your knees. Begin with eight repetitions and work to 15.*

- **Bicycle:** *Sit on an armless chair, grasp the sides with your hands, and raise your legs off the floor and pedal as if you were riding a bicycle. Attempt to keep legs as high as possible. Pedal, pedal. Attempt to go for 20 seconds and then take a brief (10 seconds) breather, and repeat. Begin with eight repetitions and work up to 15.*

- **Stand up and sit:** Sit in a sturdy chair to the count of two, then stand up and count to two again, sit down, and then stand up again. Begin with eight repetitions and work up to 15.

- **Toe raises on book:** This exercise can be done either on a sturdy book or a block of wood. Hold on to a chair for balance, and place your toes on the edge of the book or block of wood. Now, lower your heels to the floor, hold for a count of two, then lift your heels up off the floor as high as you can, trying to stand on your toes for a count of two. Begin with eight repetitions and work up to 15.

  Do you feel as if your body needs help in specific areas? Following are a few more exercises tailored to meet specific body-area needs:

- **Posture:** The first lesson every actor learns is to move with the ribcage high, shoulders back, chin and tummy in, buttocks tucked under. It's all automatic with a high rib cage.

- **Waist:** Try sit-ups or double-leg raises while sitting in your chair. Also try side bends sitting or standing, or simply draw in your waist 10 to 12 times during the day.

- **Bust:** Pushups are the best. If you can't do a full one, try a half one with your knees on the floor.

- **Thighs:** To trim and firm, try jumping leg lunges or splits, or lie on the floor on your side and do leg raises (lift and hold one leg in the air, then bring the other to meet it).

- **Buttocks:** Standing and holding on to a chair for balance, stand tall with waist in, then arch your *back and put your left leg straight back—don't bend it—then try it with the right leg. Repeat and do at least 10 repetitions for each leg.*

Exercising: Tips and Tricks

- Before starting any exercise program, always check with your physician.

- Always start by setting a goal. Everyone is different, as are their abilities. Whether your goal is to run a marathon or walk around the block, it's your goal. Aim for it, achieve it, set another goal, achieve it, and so on. Virtually anyone at any age can be fit and feel their best. All it takes is exercise.

- Start out easily, far below your capacity, and then build up your strength and stamina and do more along the way.

- Take ample rest periods between exercises in the beginning. Then, after a couple of weeks, rest only as long as it would take to complete one exercise.

- Warm up gradually.

- Be sure all your movements are full and complete.

- Exercise in a place where there's abundant fresh air, preferably outdoors or where the windows are open.

- While exercising, wear something loose and comfortable so your movements aren't hindered.

- Work out in front of a mirror so you can concentrate on the part of the body being exercised. (It's also a great way to see how you perform each movement.)

- Keep a record of your progress. Weigh yourself only once a week.

- Pay attention to your posture. Stand tall, head erect, stomach in, chest out, shoulders back.

- Try to do something every day, if possible.

- Never hold your breath while doing an exercise. Breathing should be free and unhampered.

Calories Expended Per Hour

Following are estimates of the approximate number of calories burned per hour by a 150-pound person doing various activities*:

Moderate Physical Activity	*Calories/hour*
Hiking	*370*
Light gardening/yard work	*330*
Dancing	*330*
Golf (walking w/clubs)	*330*
Walking (3.5 mph)	*280*
Weight-lifting (light workout)	*220*
Stretching	*180*
Vigorous Physical Activity	
Running/jogging (5 mph)	*590*
Bicycling (10 mph)	*590*
Swimming (slow, freestyle)	*510*
Aerobics	*480*
Walking (4.5 mph)	*460*
Heavy yard work (chopping wood)	*440*
Weight-lifting (vigorous effort)	*440*
Basketball (vigorous)	*440*

*Those who weigh less will burn fewer calories; those who are heavier, more calories.

Source: *U.S. Department of Agriculture* (www.mypyramid.gov)

Jogging, Walking, Swimming, Cycling, and More

Keep in mind that most of today's world-class athletes work out with weights, or at the very least supplement their specialty sport with systematic exercise. A sport or activity combined with weightlifting is the best way to regain good muscle tone. Even if you're not an Olympic-class athlete, consider a well-rounded regimen as that insurance policy for a healthy, long life.

Let's take a closer look at a few of the more common fitness activities.

Running/jogging. This is one of the easiest forms of fitness available. You can do it almost anywhere, anytime— just don't forget to stretch first. If you opt to join the 30-million-plus runners in the United States, it's a good idea to check with your doctor first, as you would before starting any exercise program.

Don't scrimp when it comes to buying running shoes either. A good pair that fit and are cushioned well can go a long way toward lessening the risk of impact injuries such as shin splints, bone fractures, and more—plus they just plain make it easier on your body.

Start off easily enough that you can hold a conversation while you run. Remember the make-haste-slowly story from earlier? Run only as long as you feel comfortable.

Walking. For those who don't like to or want to run, or can't physically handle the high impact, vigorous walking can be a great form of aerobic activity. In addition to the physical benefits of improving muscles and raising cardiovascular efficiency, walking is a terrific stress-reliever. Try it for a few days and you'll notice the difference.

We're not talking about a leisurely stroll. Set your mind to it and get out there and move along. My wife, Elaine, has written a book about my form of dynamic walking, Dynastride (SM), which I devised almost 60 years ago! The book, *Dynastride! Elaine LaLanne's Complete Walking Program for Fitness After 50* (The Stephen Greene Press, 1988) is a great resource for anyone, but especially those age 40 and up.

Steps to Dynastride (SM)

- *Stretch first before heading out. (See our stretches previously.)*

- *Exaggerate standing tall.*

- *Draw in your waist as tightly as you can.*

- *Swing your arms in motion with your legs.*

- *As you take a stride, swing your arms back and forward, even over your head as far as they'll go.*

When most people walk, they don't really use their arms. But by using them properly, you can improve your posture, firm up the shoulders and chest, and get great cardiovascular benefit. With Dynastriding, rather than an easy stride, the length of each stride increases so that it taxes the leg, hip, and back muscles, as well as the ligaments, tendons, and joints.

Swimming. You've heard it dozens of times: Swimming is one of the best all-around exercises. And it's true. It's a great way to tone all those muscles in your body. Because you're in the water, you get the benefits of aerobic activity without the stress and impact of other vigorous activity.

Check out the LaLanne Website (*www.jacklalanne.com*) for more information on his water exercises, Hydronastics.

Cycling. We all did it as kids. Many of us, with or without our own kids, have taken it up as adults too. If you ride with regular cadence, you'll aerobically help yourself get fit. Resistance is key. The harder your ride, the more calories you burn and the less fat you carry.

When you head out for that bike ride, you may want to consider the following:

- One way to lesson sore behinds from long rides is to wear specially padded underwear as well as getting special seats. The extra cost is worth it.

- If you have balance issues, try a bicycle with more than two wheels or one that holds more than one person. Don't overlook pedal-powered four-wheeled carts either. Choose the bike that's right for you.

- Always wear a helmet (make sure it's the right fit) and proper protection when riding.

- If you're riding at night, make sure your bike is well-lit and visible, especially if riding in traffic. Wear light-colored clothing.

Breathing and Exercise

Breathing is the elixir of life. You can do without water for days, but you can't do without oxygen for more than a few minutes. Because the air is so polluted with dust and smoke today, it's best to inhale through your nose and exhale through your mouth. When you inhale, the tiny hairs in your nose act as a filtering system.

As we age, if we don't exercise, our lung capacity shrinks and it becomes harder to take full breaths. Too many people take shallow breaths in the upper chest. Instead, when you inhale, let the diaphragm drop down so that you breathe from your lower stomach. Feel the air almost touch your back? The more you exercise, the more you breathe and the more efficient your lungs become. The oxygen you take in also helps burn fat, so keep breathing for health and well-being.

Do You Need a Trainer?

A personal trainer is the best way to motivate yourself to get with the program. It can be an expensive alternative, but if you can afford it, invest in yourself! It's worth it.

If you just don't have the money or don't want to spend it, many fitness centers offer low membership fees and classes with physical instructors. The YMCA is also a great resource, and offers a variety of exercises and exercise programs for people of all ages, at little or no cost. Ditto with local recreation and senior centers.

Invest in Yourself

The best investment any of us can make is spending the time to take care of the most important person in the world: ourselves. We do that by exercising every day and putting the right fuel in our bodies, which increases our energy levels and our vitality.

Too many people live their lives with all their aches and pains. Why not invest in yourself so that you feel good all the time and can enjoy life?

Remember, your bank account and health account are similar. The more you put in, the more you can take out!

Don't Get Discouraged

If you're not seeing the visible, physical results of your changed lifestyle fast enough, don't be discouraged. Even if you haven't lost any weight or inches for a couple of weeks, definitely don't give up on your exercise regimen or your healthful diet. Everyone reaches little fitness improvement plateaus periodically. Plus, whether it shows or not, your body is changing and improving. You're firming up, stimulating circulation, increasing lung capacity, and enjoying life more.

After you reach your goals, don't quit! Stick with your newfound physical fitness and challenge yourself with new goals. For your health's sake, for vanity's sake, for your family's sake, and for your financial future's sake, stay in shape. And remember, daily exercise is a must. Plan for it, and do it. The rewards will be well worth it.

Roadmap to Success

Physical fitness takes commitment to exercise just as it requires good nutrition. But it doesn't have to be painful. Just the opposite: vigorous exercise actually is stimulating. It boosts your energy levels, invigorates your mind, and just feels good afterward. The hardest part, of course, is getting started and keeping it up. Do it today. Invest in yourself now and reap the dividends day after day after month after year.

Here are a few easy steps to get you started, no matter your age group:

- Before you get started, stand in front of a mirror to assess your body and its health. Be honest. This is, after all, about helping yourself feel better physically and mentally.
- Physical fitness isn't necessarily about your weight only. Start by taking your measurements with a tape measure, and write down the results. Periodically retake your measurements to assess your progress *and* as incentive to see how exercise and nutrition do truly make a difference.
- Do some form of exercise daily, and regularly.
- Always stretch before exercising. Try doing it before you get out of bed in the morning. It's a great pick-me-up to start the day.
- Vary that routine every three weeks to work different muscle groups and so you don't get bored.

- Your options abound. Walk (as in vigorous). Dynastride (SM) is even better. Try bicycling, jogging, or swimming, too.

More Resources

- American Council on Exercise (*www.acefitness.org*): San Diego, California-based nonprofit; click on "Get Fit" for tips, recipes, exercises, and more.
- American College of Sports Medicine (*www.acsp.org*): The largest sports medicine and exercise science organization in the world. Click on "Resources for General Public" for information on research, fitness, consumer products, exercise equipment, and more.
- American Heart Association (*www.americanheart.org*): Click on the nonprofit's "Healthy Lifestyle" for loads of information on fitness, diet, nutrition, and health.
- Medline Plus (*medlineplus.gov*): From the National Institutes of Health and the U.S. National Library of Medicine. Click on "Health Topics" and then read on; be sure to check out information under "Health and Wellness."
- Weight Control Information Network (*win.niddk.nih.gov*): This site is an information service of the National Institute of Diabetes and Digestive Kidney Diseases, in conjunction with the National Institutes of Health and U.S. Department of Health and Human Services. Click on "For the Public" under "Publications" to access publications and resources on nutrition, physical activity, and weight control listed by subject.

Chapter 5

Step 3: Think *Positive*—

You Can Reverse

the Aging Process

Think of the glass of life as half full instead of half empty!

—Jack LaLanne

Never underestimate the power of positive thinking. If you think you can, you can. If you think you can't, you can't—and you won't! Whether you're focusing on nutrition or exercise, saving or investing, living a full life or a mediocre one, your attitude often determines your outcome. Thinking *positive* and thinking *young* is an investment in your health. If you think you're old, you *are* old. If you think *young*, studies show that you're improving your chances of a longer life—by nearly a decade, in fact.

Instead of moping around, dwelling on how *old* you are, bemoaning those aches and pains, fretting about the things you can no longer do, why not channel that energy into thinking about how young you are and how much life is still yours to live? Envision the great experiences yet in store for you. Visualization is one of the first steps toward creating a new reality. Positive thinking and visualization can revitalize and rejuvenate you instead of enervating and draining you. Don't be surprised if you retard or even reverse the effects of the aging process too, as you enjoy life more and discover a new vibrancy. After all, the glass is half full, not half empty!

Remember that *"usta"* person we talked about earlier, that person who always laments that he or she *used to* be able to do this and that? With the guidance of this book, you are increasing your chances of becoming a physically and fiscally fit *"I can"* person instead of a *"usta"* one.

Mental Commitment

The rewards of positive thinking about aging can be great. A Yale University study found that those people who have positive attitudes toward aging actually lived 7.5 years longer than those who did not. And that's accounting for age, gender, socioeconomic status, health, and loneliness. Even lower blood pressure or lower cholesterol levels can't do that much.

Arnie, the widower we talked about in the last chapter, was wasting away mentally and physically, in large part because he had quit thinking positively. After his wife died, Arnie focused on how old he was, how worn out he felt, and how he just didn't have the energy to do anything anymore. But then he received a wake-up call courtesy of *The Jack LaLanne Show* reruns on late-night TV. The show motivated him to try a little exercise, which made him feel a little better. So he exercised a little more, and felt better still. As Arnie discovered the joy of feeling better through exercise, his body and his attitude changed. He recognized that we're all capable of achieving better health, no matter our age. With a renewed and vigorous can-do attitude, Arnie reversed his debilitating downward aging spiral.

Lawrence, however, wasn't as lucky. His wife didn't die, but his career did. A successful contract consultant at age 76, Lawrence had resisted retirement for more than a decade. He enjoyed his work and its mental challenge. "Retirement was for *old* people," he always said. Until he retired, he hadn't included himself in that mix. Finally, though, he gave into family pressure and retired. His wife and grown kids had told him for years he should quit working and "take it easy."

Although Lawrence always had been extremely active and played golf weekly, rain or shine, suddenly he decided he should slow down. After all, golf could be strenuous, and he was retired, which meant he was "old." He lost his positive, youthful outlook on life.

It wasn't long before the mental and physical inactivity caught up with Lawrence. He found himself shuffling along and sitting around a lot. One day he tripped on the stairs and fell, injuring his back and requiring surgery. Two surgeries later, unwilling to exercise mentally or physically, Lawrence found himself facing the prospect of assisted living or a nursing home. And it had been only two years since his retirement.

> *Anything in life is possible, and you can make it happen.*
>
> *—Jack LaLanne*

No matter our age, we all must believe in ourselves, invest in ourselves, and have the faith, the pride, and the discipline to carry on and carry through. Chances are, all of us know someone who, despite dire circumstances, attacked a problem with a positive attitude and won. What about the newly divorced mom who hasn't had to support herself in years and suddenly finds herself solely responsible not only for her own life but for her two children as well? Sitting around bemoaning her fate won't get the job done, but a positive attitude can go a long way toward helping her rebuild her life. In this book, we've talked about those who prevail and those who don't. Attitude has much to do with success or failure in whatever we do.

Self-Worth

At times, all of us are prone to putting ourselves down. It's an unfortunate aspect of human nature that we are at times beset by doubt, fear, and insecurity, and don't see how we can possibly measure up. Some typical comments when in this negative state are:

- I'm so ugly.
- I'm too fat.
- I'm not well-educated.
- I don't make enough money.
- I'm too uncoordinated.
- I'm too old.
- I'm too frail.

The list of self-putdowns goes on and on. Just listing those negative statements is depressing. What happened to the power of positive thinking? What happened to the "I can" approach?

An essential ingredient in achieving your goals of physical (and fiscal) fitness is self-acceptance. If you don't like yourself or have faith in your ability to do something, how can you expect anyone else to like you or have faith in you?

Let's suppose that you're overweight. Who made you that way? You did, by neglecting yourself and by exercising poor nutrition choices. If you're out of shape, how did you get that way? Could it be that you don't exercise and spend most of your time parked in front of the TV drinking beer or pop? Who made those choices? It's the same when it comes to your finances. If you procrastinate and are unprepared for the future, whose fault is that? You have to shoulder the blame, accept responsibility for your situation, and regroup.

> *Author, positive thinker extraordinaire, and good friend Dr. Norman Vincent Peale would always tell me, "Jack, you should have been a preacher!" And I joked, "Norman, you're for the hereafter; I'm for the here now!"*
>
> *—Jack LaLanne*

The first step in getting your life, your body, or your finances back on track is to dump that "I can't" attitude and attack the problem head-on with a positive attitude. Pat yourself on the back and think of all your good qualities. Then get out and do it, whatever "it" is! Whether exercising, eating right, or organizing your finances, think "Every day in every way I am getting better and better. I can do anything."

For those who doubt the benefits of positive thinking, consider that renowned positive thinker Dr. Norman Vincent Peale has sold literally tens of millions of copies of his books, including *The Power of Positive Thinking*.

Another great positive thinker was Duke Kahanamoku, a native Hawaiian who often has been dubbed the father of modern surfing. He also won gold and silver medals in the 1916, 1920, and 1924 Olympics in the 100-meter freestyle swim. Kahanamoku was a quiet man with a simple but powerful message: "Practice, practice, practice using both mind and spirit!" That's a profound approach to daily life and something to remember as you lift each weight or swim each lap.

> *My favorite song is "I Believe," and I sing it at many functions and lectures. It's a positive, uplifting song that gets to the core of my philosophy of living.*

Believing in yourself in good times and in bad is one of the most uplifting things you can do in your life to effect positive change. You will be positive in good times, and optimistic in bad times.

—Jack LaLanne

Signs of Depression

Following is a checklist of signs and symptoms of clinical depression,* according to Mental Health America, formerly the National Mental Health Association:

- *Persistent sad, anxious, or "empty" mood.*

- *Changes in sleep patterns.*

- *Reduced appetite and weight loss, or increased appetite and weight gain.*

- *Loss of pleasure and interest in once-enjoyable activities, including sex.*

- *Restlessness, irritability.*

- *Persistent physical symptoms, such as chronic pain or digestive disorders that do not respond to treatment.*

- *Difficulty concentrating at work or in school, or in remembering things or making decisions.*

- *Fatigue or loss of energy.*

- *Feeling guilty, hopeless, or worthless.*

- *Thoughts of suicide or death.*

*For more information, contact Mental Health America (www.nmha.org), or your local Mental Health Association.

Depression is an illness, and it's treatable as such. Clinical depression is not caused by what you do or don't put in your mouth.

Moods, on the other hand, can be affected by diet. Many people try to manage their moods—either consciously or not—through food, often by eating more sweets or snacks. But too much sugar can actually lower energy levels. When that happens, people tend to eat even more. If they're eating the wrong kinds of food, their energy levels drop some more. It's a vicious cycle that's self-perpetuating—not to mention fattening.

Instead of heading to the snack bar or refrigerator when your mood takes a dive, develop habits that make you feel upbeat, alive, and self-assured. Try to focus on positive thinking to feel good about yourself. Exercise is a great way to stimulate those positive feelings!

Here's one individual's story:

I finally made the decision to seek professional help for my depression and substance abuse, and overcame those problems. With time, and with the willingness to be helped and to help myself, I started to gain belief in myself, hope for my life, and the confidence to become stronger in every way. As I felt better in my own head, I gained more energy. As I became more physically active and took better care of my nutritional needs, my physical health improved. As I learned to love myself, I could extend love to others, thus forming strong, healthy, and loving relationships. Because I was able to relate to people better and had more energy and desire to go to work, I was finally able to keep a secure job. And of course, financial health and freedom has followed.

If you think you have true clinical depression (see pull-out on page 122), it's important to talk to your medical professional about it and get the necessary help. If, as is the case with many people as they age, your issues are simply the result of a negative attitude, here's a way to help yourself: Make a checklist of your thoughts about aging and your age. On one side of a piece of paper, write down your negative thoughts, and on the opposite side, list positive thoughts to combat the negative ones. For example, if you feel down about life in general, think about how much you've learned through your experiences throughout the years.

And, of course, keep exercising, because if you feel better physically, you'll feel better mentally too.

Enhance Your Mental Fitness

Some ways to fight depression and stay mentally fit include:

- *Seek professional help for your depression. A doctor or other health professional can decide if you need medication and help you practice positive methods of dealing with feelings and emotions through therapy. They can also help you get to know yourself better.*

- *Educate yourself about depression. Knowing that it has different causes helps to remind us that it is not our fault. Understanding that we can live with depression by doing things to help ourselves feel better provides some light at the end of the tunnel.*

- *Talk with other people who have felt the same way. Strength comes from knowing we are not alone.*

- *Exercise and stay active.*

The Social Connection

No matter our age, social interaction with others helps us all feel loved and secure, whether consciously or unconsciously.

Changing demographics, with families now living hundreds and thousands of miles apart, only adds to the importance of networking and developing bonds with others nearby. Without relationships and connections, a person becomes isolated and can develop depression.

Edward, 81, and Helena, 78, had retired. Their children and grandchildren were scattered across the country, so they decided to move from South Dakota to Arizona. They left a lifetime of friends and memories behind. But because they chose to move to a retirement community, they interact daily with dozens of their peers and take part in many social and sports activities. The activities keep them physically active and mentally alert. Networking with so many people and participating in daily activities also helps them avoid "sitting around wasting away," and keeps them happy and fit.

At the opposite end of the spectrum, remember Lawrence, who retired and quit doing everything he previously had enjoyed? No one died, but he literally wasted away.

That can happen to anyone, at any age, in any walk of life. Depression can set in, and unless a person gets help, the downward spiral of chronic illness and ailment begins.

What You Can Do as You Age

If you have a tendency to become depressed or sad and want a pick-me-up, get active in your community. Becoming involved in a homeowners' association, local charity, or a political, study, or social group is a great way to lift you out of yourself and make a difference to others at the same time.

When Beth was 74, she moved into an apartment complex and joined its homeowners' association. The group was doing a lousy job, so, undaunted by her age and with the urging of friends, she ran for president of the association, and won. That was six years ago. She's still running the association today, and, at age 80, recently was reelected for another term. It's all about the power of positive thinking and doing what you know you can do if only you try.

Mort, then 66, retired, and a widower, had no family nearby, but with the urging of a friend decided to volunteer to help his local Meals on Wheels, the meal-delivery program for the elderly and homebound. That was four years ago. Today he's still delivering food to the homebound, and instead of feeling that he has no purpose, he gets up every morning proud and pleased that his newfound homebound friends need him and count on him.

Brenda, 46, didn't like her job. She was sickly and lonely, and never went out after work. Then one day, quite by accident, she heard about a volunteer outdoor program that built handicap-accessible trails in parks across her state. She had always liked the outdoors, so on a whim called the group and signed up to help them the following Saturday. Of course, once she got out, got involved with others, and started doing something she enjoyed, her health improved, and so did her social life and attitude. She began to exercise, eat right, and enjoy life to the fullest.

Mental fitness, similar to physical and fiscal fitness, doesn't happen overnight. But it will happen to you with the right attitude and approach.

Don't overlook participating in religious-related activities either. For some they can be a great way to get involved, regain a sense of purpose, and stay on the right attitude track.

If your problems stem from true clinical depression, you won't solve them right away. But with the proper treatment and help, combined with mild exercise, you will feel a little better day by day. Let your family and friends help you too.

Active Minds

An active mind gets stronger as it matures. Don't ever forget that. Don't let your mind waste away. Instead, present it with new challenges so it can continue to grow and function. Think about Beth, the president of her homeowners' association at age 80. She's diminutive and hardly someone you would think could handle building contractors, errant tenants, and more, but she does so, and with ease. No mental idleness for her!

Stimulate your mind!

—Jack LaLanne

Mental stimulation is a key to keeping the mind active. That means read a book, listen to classical and other genres of music, enjoy a game of chess, or try crossword puzzles. Consider learning a foreign language or even heading back to school. Take a class at a local community college or volunteer for any of the many local, regional, national, or international nonprofit organizations. Travel and learn about your town, state, country, or the world.

Knitting a simple scarf in your spare time isn't enough, and certainly plopping yourself down in front of the television for hours on end won't cut it either. No matter your age, you need to prod your brain to work overtime to solve problems and understand issues.

Even a good run [or Dynastride (SM) walk!] can help stimulate your mind, because it clears your thoughts and provides a different perspective on various situations.

An inactive mind, on the other hand, bogs down with the problems of the day—whether they're petty situations or various aches, pains, and ailments. Just as with a negative attitude, an inactive mind leads to the downward spiral of poor health and fading well-being. Think *positive* and boost your physical health, mental health, and—as you'll learn more about in the next pages—your financial health too.

Roadmap to Success

A positive outlook on life, and on aging especially, actually may prolong your life, and significantly, too. No matter your age, look for ways to keep your mind active and yourself in the social stream to help minimize depression and other debilitating ailments.

A mantra of positive thinking that applies across age groups: If you're bored, lonely, or just down in the dumps, get up, get out, and get involved. Volunteer or join a community group or club, eat right, and exercise. An active mind is a healthy mind, and even can mean a healthier body too.

More Resources

- American Heart Association (*www.americanheart .org*): Click on "Publications and Resources" or "Healthy Lifestyle" for information and pointers on the mental benefits of an active mind and physical activity.

- Mental Health America (*www.nmha.org*): Formerly known as the National Mental Health Association, it's the nation's oldest organization addressing all aspects of mental health and mental illness; offers links to its hundreds of affiliates around the country as well as information, assistance, education, and direction on mental health issues.

- Medline Plus (*www.medlineplus.gov*): Provides health information from the U.S. National Library of Medicine and the National Institutes of Health; click on "NIH SeniorHealth" for senior-specific issues and answers.

PART III

Financial Fitness for Your Future

Chapter 6

Plan Ahead—

The Peace of Mind and

Financial Security Is Worth It

> *By creating peace of mind, you are creating quality of life.*
>
> —*Matt Rettick*

Now that you're on the right track to good physical and mental health and long life, it's time to get your financial house in shape too. After all, you don't want your money to run out before you do. The right kind of financial planning also provides the peace of mind that *if* something does happen to you or a loved one in the future, you've planned for it and are prepared. Without proper planning, you likely will end up at the mercy of charity.

> *If you don't pay attention daily to your body, you won't live long. If you don't pay attention to your finances, your money won't last long. And if you don't do either, you're at the mercy of charity.*
>
> —*Matt Rettick*

In case you think you don't need to be prepared for the future, you better think again. Statistics are *not* in your favor.

Remember that health and financial crisis we talked about in Chapter 1, and those physical realities LaLanne has pointed out? Let's revisit the statistics:

- Often-preventable chronic diseases such as heart disease, cancer, and stroke account for the vast majority of deaths of those aged 65 and up.

- 64.5 percent of U.S. adults are overweight or obese and as a result are at increased risk of serious illnesses and diseases.

- By 2020, one in six Americans will be 65 or older. That's almost 55 million people, or 16.5 percent of the total population (U.S. General Accounting Office numbers, testimony by David M. Walker, U.S. comptroller general, before Senate Special Committee on Aging, March 21, 2002).

- The vast majority of seniors don't have enough assets to pay for a year of nursing-home care. Consider these statistics from "The Distribution of Assets in the Elderly Population Living in the Community" (#7335), The Henry J. Kaiser Family Foundation, June 2005:

  - Two-thirds of elderly people living in the community have resources equal to less than one year of the cost of nursing-home care ($70,000).

  - The majority of elderly in this range have very low asset levels.

  - 57 percent have assets below $5,000, less than the cost of one month of nursing-home care.

  - 19 percent of elderly people living in the community have assets equal to three or more years of the average cost of nursing-home care.

- If you think Medicare will pick up the tab for your extended long-term care, you're mistaken.

It doesn't. Period (even its 100-day maximum comes with co-pays). And for Medicaid to kick in, you'll have to be practically broke. Unfortunately, more than one million people a year are forced to reach that state.

- If you're counting on your family to care for you if you become ill, take note: Changes in the typical American family, including higher divorce rates, could affect the availability of traditional family assistance and care. In 1960, 1.6 percent of males and 1.5 percent of women age 65 and older were divorced. Those numbers climbed to 7 percent and 8.6 percent, respectively, in 2003. When people in their early 60s are included in the divorced count, the figures climb to 12.2 percent of men, and 15.9 percent of women (U.S. Census Bureau report commissioned by National Institute on Aging, "65+ in the United States: 2005").

The Care Dilemma

What if you or a loved one are among those people needing care as you age? Have you planned for how you'll pay for catastrophic illness? Who will take care of you? Can you afford to pay for your care or the care of a spouse or loved one? Can your children handle that extra responsibility? Do you want your children or loved ones to feel they must shoulder that burden? Do you want to end up in a nursing home at all?

Almost half of those Americans who are married and reach age 60 will live to age 95.

—U.S. Census Data

Chances are, the answers to those questions are *no* or *not without a struggle.* Unless you're among the 19 percent of the senior population who can afford longer-term care for three years or more, you probably can't afford to pay out literally tens of thousands of dollars a year on long-term in-home or nursing-home care. Even if you have that kind of money, you'd probably much rather spend it on yourself or your family, or save it as a legacy for your heirs.

Eloise, 79, was quite comfortable financially. Never married, she had worked as a bookkeeper for the same company for more than 40 years, religiously socking away the majority of her paycheck in blue-chip stocks. By the time she retired at age 69, she had amassed more than $1 million in holdings, and was thrilled, because now she would have a solid legacy to pass on to her nieces and nephews. Growing up in the Midwest as a child of the Great Depression, she remembered many days of empty stomachs and the fear of doing without. She wanted to do her part to ensure that her family never ended up in a similar state.

Unfortunately, although Eloise planned how to create her legacy and how to distribute it, she didn't plan how to preserve it. Always healthy, she never thought to prepare for the "what-ifs" in life. At age 79, she had an unexpected massive heart attack that left her unable to care for herself. Alone in a small town far from family, she had only one option—a nursing home. She had more than enough money to cover the costs out of pocket. But before she died 12 years later, the average $5,000 a month cost of care had taken a tremendous chunk of her hard-earned savings and severely limited the legacy she had so wanted to pass on.

Remember Arnie, the frail, 62-year-old widower who discovered the LaLanne way to physical fitness and came roaring back to life? Not only did Arnie regain his health, but he woke up to the importance of being prepared for his financial future too. His short-lived frailty helped him recognize the importance of planning for health contingencies so that his children wouldn't be forced to worry about him.

And it wasn't just the logistics of care and support that prompted his awakening: "I love my kids, but they were driving me crazy. Every day, sometimes several times a day, they kept calling and stopping by and fussing after me. I'm not ready to be treated like a small child," Arnie added defiantly.

His solution was to purchase a long-term-care insurance policy. For less than $3,000 a year, he's set for life. Even if he lives to age 90, he still will have paid in only about the cost of one year's nursing-home care, and that's at today's national annual average, which doesn't take into account rising costs or inflation. Nursing-home care likely will cost a whole lot more in five, 10, or 15 years, and beyond. "It's definitely worth the expense. What else am I going to spend my money on, anyway?" he added. (We'll talk more about the details of long-term-care insurance in the next chapter.)

A Note on Risk

> *I am not so much interested in the return* on *my money as I am in the return* of *my money.*
>
> *—Will Rogers*

Life is about risk. Physically, if you don't take care of yourself, you're gambling that you won't live all that long, contract any debilitating diseases, or need expensive care. Financially, if you don't prepare, you're gambling too. Only, if you do run out of money as you age, you're left to cope anyway.

Most people can't afford to take undue risk with their hard-earned savings or principal. They need it for the future. No matter what anyone says or does to try to cajole you into investing that principal into something risky, think twice. What would happen if you *did* lose that principal? According to U.S. Census data, if you reach age 60 and are married, there's a 40 percent chance that you or your spouse will reach age 95. Can you afford to gamble that you won't be among the seniors who live that long and that you won't need that money? Probably not.

Throughout the past 20 years, inflation has averaged a little more than 3 percent annually, but we still can't afford to risk our money to beat inflation. Many Americans apparently recognize that fact. Look at the almost $4 trillion in certificates of deposit and savings accounts today (as of first quarter 2006, according to the Federal Reserve), even though their return usually doesn't keep pace with inflation. Also, what happens if you invest in CDs and need to withdraw the money before they reach full maturity? You face penalties—and you may lose part of your principal. Higher levels of risk are for younger investors!

Basically we have three phases of our financial lives, each of which calls for varying levels of risk:

1. **Accumulation phase**
    - Ages approximately 20-60
    - Moderate- to high-risk investments
2. **Preservation phase**
    - Retirement years/ages 60+
    - No risk or as little risk as possible
3. **Distribution phase**
    - Occurs at death
    - Safeguarding assets for your heirs

Risk Pyramid

The pyramid shown on the next page compares the level of risk of various investments.

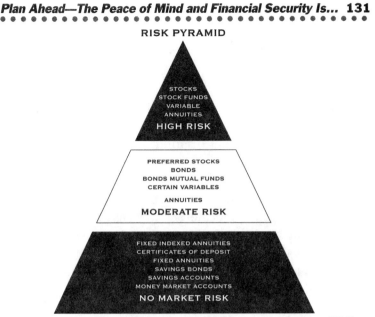

Source: Covenant Reliance Producers, LLC

Ideally, we need to pay attention to all three phases and the risks associated with each. Don't lose sight of the fact that—just as with physical fitness and exercise—keeping your principal in shape takes discipline, direction, and conviction.

If your child or grandchild is upset and wants that too-expensive toy to console him or her, don't cave in. Think of such purchases in terms of trading a potentially vital portion of your assets for something quite trivial. You are not being selfish to consider your future.

In the same vein, if Junior needs money for college, think twice, three, or four times before dipping into your nest egg to give it to him. He has many ways to fund his higher education—from scholarships to low-interest loans and more—but you have only one way to fund your retirement—you.

Investing Basics

If a pitch for an equity or stocks/bonds/mutual-funds investment is that it's a great long-term, low-risk place for your hard-earned dollars, think twice. It may be okay for a portion of your cash *after* you've invested your nest egg with security of principal in mind. Here's why.

There is a safe, sound, and profitable alternative for your nest egg that allows you to participate in stock market–linked gains without market risk to your principal. It's the fixed indexed annuity, formerly known as an equity indexed annuity, which we'll talk about later.

Beyond your nest egg, you also can, with the right money-management strategy and guidance, opt to invest that extra cash in certain investment vehicles that offer potentially higher returns and lower fees. We'll talk more about that in Chapter 9.

Financial Sharks and Savings

As we retire, we will all have four major financial concerns:

- Reducing tax liabilities: This includes capital gains taxes, Social Security taxes, income taxes, and estate taxes.

- Earning competitive interest rates on savings: This includes your personal savings as well as retirement dollars, and earning interest while reducing risk to your principal.

- Protecting savings: No matter how much money you have, you can't afford to lose it to nursing-home expenses or forced poverty via Medicaid spend-down.

- Avoiding probate and protecting your estate for your heirs: Leaving a legacy for those who follow you represents a significant goal for many.

It all sounds simple and straightforward, but of course it's not. That's because of what we refer to as the *five financial sharks* lurking nearby that feed on your finances and threaten to thwart your retirement dreams. What are those frenzied, hungry sharks?

The tax shark. We've all heard the saying, "There are only two guarantees in life: death and taxes." Death happens once; unfortunately we could be subjected to many different types of taxes during our lifetime. Do you realize that in 1948 the average family of four paid just 2 cents in taxes on every $1 they earned? In 2008, that same family paid anywhere from 10 cents to 35 cents for every dollar earned. That's up to more than one-third of your income going to Uncle Sam, and that's only for federal income tax. Most states impose their own state income taxes too. And don't overlook the sneaky taxes like Social Security taxes, sales taxes, excise taxes, Medicare taxes, capital gains taxes, vehicle taxes, road taxes, death taxes, IRA taxes... The list goes on and on.

The nursing-home shark. If you haven't planned ahead and protected yourself, what assets do you plan to liquidate first so you can get financial relief from the crippling cost of long-term care in a nursing home? The only way the government will provide help is if you qualify for Medicaid, the federal health financial assistance program for the poor. What if you really don't need or want nursing-home care? What about in-home care? What if you just need a little help with daily living?

Too bad! You could be out of luck if you haven't planned ahead for catastrophic illness protection. Cost of that care easily can top hundreds of thousands and even millions of dollars if you don't plan properly. You can also lose the right to control your own life.

The legal shark. Welcome to today's litigious world. If someone is unhappy with something, the solution seems to be to sue someone. Even your last wishes as expressed in your will could be at risk of being torpedoed by a legal challenge. If not derailed by a lawsuit, your wishes certainly could be delayed by the legal, time-consuming hassles of probate court (the legal process your will must go through after you die and before your assets are distributed).

The investment shark. Should you put your money in the bank (as in CDs and money-market accounts) or in the stock market (as in equities and mutual funds)? Markets go up and markets go down; so do interest rates. Can you afford to risk losing any of your principal? If your goal is peace of mind and security, the answer should be no when it comes to your nest egg. Beyond that, certain money management investment strategies can maximize returns with minimal fees and taxes.

The procrastination shark. It's that put-off-today-what-you-can-do-tomorrow syndrome. We all fall victim to it, whether out of fear of change or just plain habit. Whatever the reasons for delaying catastrophic illness-planning or getting fit physically, the end result is the same: You're ill-prepared for the future, or you wake up too late to the realities of what you should have done and didn't.

Change can be a good thing. Look at how change has made our lives so much easier: The horse and buggy gave way to the automobile, the telegraph to the telephone, and the outhouse to inside plumbing and flush toilets. Can you imagine washing mounds of dirty clothes on a scrub board in a stream instead of dumping the laundry into a washing machine?

Look at planning for your financial future as a positive move, and that may help you get the job done. It's that LaLanne power of positive thinking again.

Affording the Solution

With long-term care costs in the stratosphere and still climbing, the affordability issue has new meaning. Unless you're among the very wealthy, can you afford not to prepare for long-term-care contingencies? It just makes sense to spend a little today to save astronomical amounts later.

Remember Louise, the 55-year-old widow from earlier in the book who bought long-term-care insurance? She opted to buy the insurance now so that she wouldn't have to burden her grown children later. It was an easy choice for her. By buying the insurance at a relatively young age, Louise was able to get an affordable premium that should stay constant once the policy is purchased.

> *Can you afford NOT to plan for catastrophic illness as you age? The cost is a few dollars a day to save hundreds of thousands of dollars later.*
>
> *—Matt Rettick*

If you still think long-term-care insurance or some other catastrophic-illness planning is out of your financial reach or takes too much effort, read on. In the next chapters we'll show you just how easy it is to be fiscally fit and prepared for your financial future.

Financial Advisors

"Do it yourself" is a way of life for many people who don't like to pay others or turn to them for help, no matter what needs to be done. That's fine for painting the kitchen or changing the oil in your car. But your financial future is one aspect of your life that you need to get right the first time. After all, the quality of your life and that of your loved ones is on the line.

Just as your physical body changes as it ages, so do your financial needs, concerns, and approaches to risk. The right professional advisor—one who specializes in retirement planning—can help you make the right decisions to avoid the financial sharks and address your financial concerns. He or she can guide you through the confusing and often convoluted areas of financial, estate, healthcare, and long-term-care planning, and can help you sort through the ins and outs of Medicare and the many choices of Medicare supplemental policies before you're in crisis mode. The right advisor not only can help you understand the unique risks of various investments at the different stages of your life, but can also identify local resources and ideal investments to save you time and money, and avoid unnecessary hassles in the long run.

Be careful though. Many people may claim they're financial advisors, but all are not equally qualified. Pay attention to any potential advisor's credentials, experience, and references. A number of professional organizations offer free online or offline locator services (see More Resources on page 145 for sources).

Roadmap To Success

Even if you're a do-it-yourselfer, when it comes to your financial future, it's best to bring in an expert for advice and guidance, because a mistake truly can have dire consequences for you and your loved ones.

Life is about risks—what's acceptable and what's not. When it comes to investing, higher levels of risk are for younger investors. But everyone, no matter their age, should pay attention to the levels of risk associated with various stages in their financial lives:

- **Accumulation** (ages 20–60): Moderate- to high-risk investments
- **Preservation** (ages 60+): No risk or as little risk as possible

- **Distribution** (at death): Safeguarding assets for heirs

More Resources

- Covenant Consumer Resource Center (*www .covenantresource.com*): A consumer-oriented Website from Matt Rettick and his Covenant Reliance Producers team dedicated to helping preretirees and retirees access the necessary information to safeguard their estates and become financially fit for life; check out the free booklets available on a variety of topics.
- Financial Planning Association (*www.fpanet .org*): Click on "Public/Find a Planner" for lots of information and helpful articles on financial planning; click on "PlannerSEARCH.org" to find a planner near you.
- National Academy of Elder Law Attorneys (*www.naela.org*): Click on "Public," and then "Resources" for explanations on a variety of topics, including long-term care, elder law attorneys, and more; click on "NAELA Directory" to find an elder law attorney.

Chapter 7

Step 4: Insure Your Future—

Long-Term-Care Insurance,

Modified Endowment

Contracts, and More

You want to be sure that your money doesn't run out before you do.

—Matt Rettick

Insurance is about protecting against risk. You insure your home against the risk of fire, theft, and natural disasters; your car against the risk of accident; your health against the financial risk of high out-of-pocket medical expenditures via health insurance. So why not insure yourself against the risk that you'll need some kind of long-term care or help in the future?

After all, as we've talked about, the odds are against you. Still not convinced that you could and likely will need some long-term care at some point? Let's put it another way:

- The odds that you'll ever use your homeowner's insurance are one in 80 ("LTC Insurance is still a Tough Sell Despite Many New Features," National Underwriters, May 10, 1999).

- The odds are one in 40 that you'll use your automobile insurance (also National Underwriters).

- If you're post-retirement age, the odds that you'll need some kind of long-term care are about one in three (Peter Kemper, Harriet Komisar, and Lisa Alexcih, "Long-Term Care over an Uncertain Future: What can Current Retirees Expect?" *Inquiry* 2006).

Again, it just makes sense to insure your future. Remember too that of everyone who is 65 today, 35 percent will spend more than five years in a nursing home! (Kemper, Komisar, and Alexcih.) Do you have the tens of thousands and hundreds of thousands of dollars to foot that bill out of pocket? Or have you planned how you'll qualify for Medicaid without hurting your loved ones in the present and future? Again, for most Americans, the answer to those questions is no.

The biggest shortcoming of long-term care in general is that people just don't understand how fast its cost is growing, says Phyllis Shelton, a nationally recognized long-term-care insurance authority and president of Nashville, Tennessee–based LTC Consultants (*www.ltcconsultants.com*).

Factoring in inflation, the cost of your future care, if it's required, is mind-boggling. Consider a few numbers from Shelton, author of *Long-Term Care: Your Financial Planning Guide* (LTCi Publishing, 2007): The average annual cost of care today is $75,000—and that's not 'round-the-clock care. It's eight to 10 hours of daily home care or a private room in a facility. With the accepted inflation rate for care costs at about 6 percent, that means the cost of care will triple in 20 years. If you're 50 years old today and project that growth rate out 30 years, you'll have to pay about $32,000 a month, or $310,000 a year!

Long-term-care insurance with inflation protection is the easiest and most thorough way to ensure that you're prepared for such contingencies. It's also the most widely recognized solution. Long-term-care insurance is a policy that—in exchange for your premiums—will cover the cost of your care (generally with limitations and exclusions) in a variety of settings and for varying lengths of time up to the rest of your life.

If you can't afford long-term-care insurance or can't qualify because of a preexisting health condition, other insurance alternatives that might provide your financial solution include:

- Modified endowment contracts, or MECs: This basically is an over-funded life insurance policy with a high cash value that you can use as a living benefit if and when you become chronically ill and need the money to pay for long-term care. (It still includes a residual death benefit of 10 percent of the original death benefit amount.)

- Combination annuity/long-term-care insurance policies that allow the proceeds to be used for long-term care, with any unused benefits going to a beneficiary at death.

- Life insurance policy with accelerated benefit rider. This is a life insurance policy with accelerated, or living benefits that can, under certain circumstances, allow for a portion of the benefit to be paid to the policyholder to meet long-term-care expenses.

- Life settlement/viatical settlement: A way to generate cash, in which a life insurance policy holder, if he or she becomes chronically or terminally ill, sells his or her entire policy benefit for a certain amount of cash. The amount is determined by factors including life expectancy, health condition, and more.

Each option has its advantages and disadvantages, depending on an individual's physical, financial, and health situation.

With all the options, though, pay attention to inflation and actual future needs, reminds Shelton.

Let's look more closely at what might be right for you.

Long-Term-Care Insurance

Many people have misconceptions about long-term care insurance. Let's review some of the myths that surround the need for this type of protection.

Myth No. 1

The cost of long-term care is already covered by Medicare or other medical plans.

In reality, most medical plans, including Medicare, which is available only for those 65 or older, cover very little if any long-term care, and generally only full-time care in a skilled nursing facility (usually a nursing home), and definitely not custodial care. The latter is the type of long-term care most people require that helps with what's known as activities of daily living, or ADLs. These are basic everyday tasks such as personal hygiene, mobility (transferring), bathroom duties (toileting), dressing, eating, and more. Medicare will, for example, pick up the tab for a nursing-home stay of short duration following a hospital stay, and will cover up to 100 days on a phased-out (co-pay) cost basis. But after 100 days, you'll have to pay. Medicare also covers periodic home-health visits by a qualified medical professional as prescribed by a doctor.

But what happens if you need more care after those benefits are exhausted? If you haven't prepared, you're out of luck and out of cash, too, because you're responsible for the cost. Medigap, the private insurance you buy to supplement what Medicare doesn't cover, won't pay either. Again, according to the Henry J. Kaiser Family Foundation (2004), Medicaid is the primary source of payment for approximately 58 percent of nursing-home residents. If you or an elderly loved one has no money or possessions and truly can't pay for care, Medicaid will step in and ensure that you get care, but in many cases you won't be able to get the care when and where you would like. You also could lose your privacy and/or your dignity because Medicaid doesn't pick up the cost of a private room, only a semi-private one. Also, its nursing homes are limited in numbers, as are Medicaid-designated beds in private nursing homes.

Adding to the risk, what happens if you're in an automobile accident or fall and break a bone so that you need extended care beyond what's covered under a health insurance policy (or Medicare, if you're 65 or over)? Even if you're physically fit, a perfect nutritional specimen, and as mentally sharp at age 85 as you were at 45, you could slip and fall or have an auto accident and need care. Or what if you get caught in a natural disaster?

Again, more troubling questions that call for us all to be prepared for contingencies.

Myth No. 2

Long-term care insurance covers care in a nursing home only.

Not so. Different plans cover different types of care. Some pay only for long-term care in a nursing home; others also cover long-term care you receive in your home or other settings. The best plans today cover you in four important areas: (1) home healthcare, (2) assisted living care, (3) adult day care, (4) nursing-home care.

Myth No. 3

You need long-term-care insurance only if you're wealthy with many assets to protect.

Also not true. In these days of unaffordable long-term-care costs that keep climbing every year—plus in inflation—almost everyone needs long-term-care insurance unless they absolutely have no money at all to pay for it. And what if a person doesn't really need full-time skilled nursing services and may need help only with daily living activities such as those provided at an assisted-living facility or in-home? Long-term-care insurance can pick up the tab for that too.

Myth No. 4

Most people stay in nursing homes only a short time.

Actually, statistics show that the average length of a nursing-home stay is 2.4 years, according to the National Center for Health Statistics (*The National Nursing Home Survey*, June 2002). Multiply that 2.4 years by the national average annual cost of $68,985 for a semi-private room (The MetLife Mature Market Institute numbers), and the cost of that stay is more than a whopping $160,000. If you prefer your privacy, the cost rises to more than $180,000. And that's just the average stay and the average cost. For many retirees, the cost far exceeds those numbers. In New York, for example, the average cost of a semi-private room in a nursing home is more than $121,545 a year! That's no small change for anyone of any income.

Myth No. 5

Alzheimer's disease and dementia are not covered by long-term-care insurance policies.

The truth is that today virtually all plans cover Alzheimer's or dementia if the disease develops after the coverage is in effect. Generally, companies don't offer long-term-care insurance to anyone who already has Alzheimer's or dementia at the time they apply for the policy. But even then you have options, which we'll talk about later.

Myth No. 6

Not me! I'm in great health, have good genes in my family, and I'm not going to end up needing long-term care anywhere.

We hope we've already convinced you that the numbers are stacked against you. After all, even the U.S. Department of Health and Human Services estimates that at age 65 you have at least a four in 10 (40 percent) chance of going into a nursing home at least sometime during your lifetime, and a 10 percent chance the stay will last five years or longer. At age 85, the odds climb to 55 percent.

Keep Costs Down

So forget the pipedream that it's always someone else who needs to be prepared, and look into long-term care insurance today. The time to think about it is *before* you need it. After all, as with other types of health-related insurance, you generally (though not always) need to be in good health when you apply for it. Some types of insurance and policies make exceptions for certain conditions depending on how long ago a medical event occurred. In those situations though, costs often will be higher. Policies are drawn up on an individual basis, so don't assume you can't get a certain type of coverage just because you have a chronic disease or had a heart attack 20 years ago.

Buying long-term-care insurance when you're younger is less expensive too. Louise, the widow who didn't want to burden her kids with any future care, bought her insurance at age 55 at a cost of $1,669/year. Had she waited until age 65, the premium would have gone up 270 percent for comparable coverage (that is, a policy that would pay up to nearly $122,000 in benefits when she is 80 years old), and if she didn't buy it until age 75, the cost would be 10 times as much. Her policy offers a benefit of up to $100/day for all levels of care for a five-year benefit period, which kicks in after a 90- to 100-day waiting period (usually called the elimination period), and with 5 percent compound increases in benefits each year to try to offset the effect of inflation. A similar policy for a couple at age 55 would cost $2,056/year, assuming that one of them qualifies for a preferred health discount, according to industry consultant and analyst Claude Thau. The prices are based on the assumption that the premiums are paid until the person dies or needs the policy's benefits.

The cost of premiums is expected to remain the same each year; it can increase, but not on an individual basis. For example, if a premium increase were necessary, it would have to increase for all policyholders in a certain age group, not just one particular policyholder, even if, perhaps, his or her health deteriorated. Before you buy any policy, though, always ask the insurer if they've ever increased rates for a current policyholder, and why.

Just because you're already in your 60s or 70s doesn't mean you shouldn't consider long-term-care insurance as a possible option. Having coverage, after all, even at the higher premium costs, is preferable to paying the astronomical costs of elder care out of your own pocket. This is catastrophic illness-planning by the numbers.

Don't make assumptions on prices or coverage, either, without talking to your agent.

Who Doesn't Need Long-Term-Care Insurance?

- *The very wealthy who can afford to pay for their care out of pocket.*

- *The poor who already qualify for Medicaid or can't afford the policy premiums anyway.*

Drawbacks

The disadvantages of long-term-care insurance are often colored by public misperception. For example, many people think they can't afford it. The reality, however, is this: Can you afford *not* to have it with the current national average cost of nursing-home care topping $68,985 to $77,745 annually, depending on whether a room is semiprivate or private?

Another common misperception is that you can't qualify for long-term-care insurance. Yes, it's true that some people with certain preexisting conditions within certain time frames don't qualify, but each case is unique, and you don't know for sure whether you qualify unless you try.

Another possible drawback of buying a long-term-care insurance policy is if you purchase a policy of certain duration and then need its benefits after the policy has expired. In that case, you're just out of luck.

Shop for the Right Policy

As with anything else, shop around for the right policy with the best company for your needs. Don't simply buy the first policy that comes your way. Also, be sure that if you compare policies, you compare apples to apples—comparing the same benefits, limitations, options, and more. Here's a brief look at some aspects of policy coverage to explore *before* you buy.

Daily guaranteed benefit. Make sure you know the exact amount of daily benefit that a policy guarantees. Will it be enough to meet your current needs? How much is enough? Will it cover the cost of care in your area? Simply covering the cost of the nursing home isn't enough: You'll also need to pay medical provider fees, durable goods fees, and more. How much more money will that take? In some areas, the current cost of care is $100 a day. In others, that cost could be $150 or even $350 a day. Before you shop for a policy, familiarize yourself with the cost of various levels of care in your geographic area. That should be the starting point for what you consider an acceptable daily benefit.

Inflation protection. A good policy should include automatic benefit increases to protect you from inflation. If it doesn't, as we've talked about, the daily benefit that's enough coverage today certainly won't be in five, 10, 15, and more years down the road. You should include a 5 percent inflationary factor (that means it will increase 5 percent a year even if the inflation rate is less than that) because inflation attacks everything in this country. A 5 percent *compound* rate is better than a *simple* 5 percent. Nursing homes or adult day care or home-healthcare is subject to inflation too. With the 5 percent inflationary factor, your daily benefit increases by 5 percent compounded per year. For example, Louise's $100/day benefit today will grow to $163/day in 10 years.

Elimination period. The equivalent of a deductible on a policy, this is the time period that elapses before your policy benefits kick in. Generally it's 30, 60, or 90 to 100 days. The elimination period equals the number of days you will have to pay out of pocket for your care. The longer you pay for your own care initially, the smaller your annual premiums. Many people opt for the 90-day elimination period as a way to hold down the cost of premiums.

Waiver of premium. This allows a policyholder to stop paying premiums while receiving benefits. Watch for restrictions on this clause that might require you to be in a facility a certain length of time before the waiver is granted.

What's covered? Make sure that any policy you consider covers you in *all four* important areas: home healthcare, assisted living, adult day care, and nursing-home care. It's also a good idea to purchase a policy that's a *qualified plan*, which means that when you trigger the benefits, the income you receive from the policy is not taxable to you.

Benefit triggers. Other than the elimination period, these are the specific conditions that must be met in order for your policy to begin paying you benefits. Generally they're based on the policyholder's ability to perform for him- or herself the activities of daily living, or ADLs. As we've talked about, these include things such as eating, dressing, bathing, using the bathroom, controlling body functions (continence), and mobility (also known as *transferring*).

Preexisting conditions. If you already have a health problem when you become insured, some policies may require a certain time to elapse before they will pay for care related to that preexisting condition.

Renewability. Almost all long-term-care insurance policies are guaranteed renewable and cannot be canceled as long as the premiums are paid on time and you're truthful about your health on the application. But it never hurts to make sure.

Strength of a Company

If you're a person who likes to support the little guy, the mom-and-pop businesses of the world, take note. When purchasing long-term-care insurance, consider going with the large, well-established organization with a solid performance and long-term track record. That's because with long-term-care insurance, you're not buying insurance for the present. It's insurance for the future—your future—and you want the company to be around down the road when you need it.

Insurance Company Ratings

You can check the financial soundness of an insurance company as determined by various rating agencies, including:

- *A.M. Best Company* (www.ambest.com)

- *Moody's Investors Service* (www.moodys.com)

- *Standard & Poor's (www.standardandpoors.com)*

- *Weiss Ratings Inc. (www.weissratings.com)*

Major Providers

Among the largest providers of long-term care insurance:

- *Genworth Financial (www.genworth.com)*

- *John Hancock (www.johnhancock.com)*

- *MetLife Inc. (www.metlife.com)*

- *Allianz Group (www.allianz.com)*

The National Association of Insurance Commissioners also offers a free consumer guide to long-term-care insurance. You can order it from their Website, *naic.org.*

Pay attention to your potential longevity when looking for solutions to possible long-term-care funding needs too, adds Shelton. If people in your family tend to live to age 90 and beyond, make sure that you're potentially covered for that long, and that your inflation benefit continues as well. (With some policies, inflation benefits stop growing after a certain length of time, with the end result that you may not have enough inflation protection if you live another 10 to 15 years.)

Partnership for Long-Term-Care Programs

We'll talk more about Medicaid and what it covers in Chapter 11. But basically, the Medicaid Long-Term-Care Partnership Program is a public-private funding program for long-term care in several states (the number is growing, including California, Connecticut, Indiana, and New York), that enables seniors to hang on to a chunk of their assets and still get Medicaid if they purchase a qualifying long-term-care insurance policy. The program began as an experiment in reducing Medicaid expenses by delaying or eliminating the need for some people to rely on Medicaid to pick up the long-term cost of care by purchasing qualifying long-term-care insurance policies. Insurers then would pick up initial costs of long-term care for policyholders. When and if additional funding is needed to pay the cost of care, Medicaid then kicks in without forcing a spend-down of assets to the poverty level, as normally required to qualify for Medicaid.

Now, thanks to the Budget Deficit Reduction Act of 2005, more states are allowed to offer this voluntary program as well.

In operation since the 1990s, the program has enabled almost 212,000 total policies to be purchased. Today more than 172,000 partnership policies remain active in the four states, according to General Accounting Office estimates.

Investments Versus Insurance

One typical excuse for not buying long-term-care insurance is, "I can do better investing the money myself." This is the time to rethink that approach.

Investing the money instead of buying a long-term-care insurance policy can't cut it as a solution to future care costs. If, instead of paying insurance premiums every year, you invested that same amount, you couldn't make anywhere close to enough money to cover the cost of your care. A scenario from the nonprofit Insurance Information Institute shows why:

Let's say you're age 55 and invest $2,000 a year—the approximate cost of a long-term-care insurance premium—at 5 percent a year net after taxes for 30 years. (We're assuming, theoretically, that you won't need the money for at least 30 years, and we won't even discuss what would happen if you need the money before age 85!) At the end of those 30 years, *and* with the magic of compounding, your savings would have grown to $139,500. Assume that today's monthly cost of nursing-home care also grows by 5 percent a year, from $7,000 a month to $28,800 a month, due to inflation. Your 30 years of savings wouldn't even be able to fund six months in a nursing home! Of course, inflation may not rise that much; your investment could earn more—or less—and all sorts of other variables apply, but you get the picture. Long-term-care insurance is a bargain.

Checklist for a Long-Term-Care Insurance Policy

The nonprofit America's Health Insurance Plans (www.ahip.org) suggests a few questions to ask regarding any long-term-care insurance policy you're considering. (Reprinted with permission from America's Health Insurance Plans):

1. What services are covered?

- *Nursing-home care*

- *Home healthcare*

- *Assisted-living facility*

- *Adult day care*

- *Respite care*

- *Other*

2. How much does the policy pay per day for each of these?

3. How long will benefits last in a nursing home, assisted living, or other facility?

4. Does the policy have a maximum lifetime benefit? If so, what is it for nursing-home care, home healthcare, assisted living, or another facility?

5. Does the policy have a maximum length of coverage for each period of confinement? If so, what is it for each living situation?

6. How long is the waiting period before preexisting conditions are covered?

7. How long is the waiting period or "deductible" before benefits begin for nursing-home care, home healthcare, an assisted-living facility, or other?

8. Are Alzheimer's disease and other organic mental and nervous disorders covered?

9. Does the policy require an assessment of activities of daily living, cognitive impairment, physician certification of need, or a prior hospital stay for nursing- home care or home healthcare? Also, is a prior nursing-home stay required for home healthcare coverage?

10. Is the policy guaranteed renewable?

11. What is the age range for enrollment?

12. Is there a waiver of premium provision for nursing-home care or home healthcare?

13. How long must the policyholder be confined before premiums are waived?

14. Does the policy have a non-forfeiture benefit?

15. Does the policy offer an inflation adjustment feature? If so, what is the rate of increase, how often is it applied, for how long, and is there an added cost?

16. How much does the policy cost per month, per year, and with and without the inflation adjustment and non-forfeiture features?

17. Is there a 30-day free look or refund policy?

18. Has the insurance company ever had a rate increase on current policyholders? [Question recommended by Matt Rettick.]

Modified Endowment Contract

Beyond basic long-term-care insurance, insurers offer many products, variations, and combinations of coverage that provide long-term, living, life, and death benefits to meet consumers' needs. One of those different approaches to catastrophic illness planning is a Modified Endowment Contract with combination benefits.

A MEC, as it's typically called, is a life insurance policy that's over-funded up front so it typically has a high cash value that's accessible to pay for a variety of things, including costs associated with a chronic illness and need. (Any cash-value life insurance policy can be converted into a MEC as a result of how you fund it). It can be a good option if you can't afford or don't qualify for long-term-care insurance.

Additionally, an MEC that offers combination benefits can be an attractive alternative to traditional long-term-care insurance. Here's how it works:

- You deposit a single premium into the MEC universal product that has life and long-term-care benefits.

- Immediately that creates a pool of money for long-term-care expenses that's often three or four times your lump sum because of the policy's linked long-term benefit rider.

- You also immediately have a life insurance benefit that's often two to three times your lump sum premium because of the dollar value of the death benefit.

- You also have guaranteed return of premium protection, so if you ever want your money back, it's yours (no penalties and no fees).

- With this kind of a product only one of three things can happen:

- You have a long-term-care claim and use the pool of money.

- You die, and the death benefit is income-tax free, payable to your beneficiary.

- You request guaranteed return of premium and get your money back.

Even if you use up your entire pool of money for long-term-care costs, the policy has a guaranteed 10 percent residual death benefit. All of these benefits come without having to pay the cost of long-term-care premiums, either.

Consider Nancy's case. She's 65, a nonsmoker, and has put aside $300,000 for long-term care. With a single $100,000 payment, she purchases an MEC, and allocates the other $200,000 for other needs. If Nancy needs long-term care, she'll receive up to $83,203 annually for six years to reimburse monthly long-term-care costs (that's a maximum $6,934 a month). She'll receive up to a total of $499,218, income-tax free. That's nearly 500 percent of her original premium payment of $100,000.

If Nancy changes her mind and wants her money back, she notifies the insurer in writing, and they send her a check for the original $100,000, minus adjustments for any loans or previous withdrawals, no questions asked. A portion of the returned money, however, may be subject to taxation.

If Nancy never needs long-term care, the policy will provide her loves ones with a $166,406 income tax–free death benefit. If she uses only a portion of the death benefit for long-term care, the policy passes the remaining portion, income-tax free, to her beneficiaries (less any loans or withdrawals she's made).

Consider also that if you buy long-term-care insurance, you pay premiums every year and never see the money again, unless, of course, you need it. That's a lot of money out the window. If your premiums are $3,000 a year, over 20 years that's $60,000—certainly not chump change.

With an MEC, distributions are taxed like annuity distributions, thus the opportunity to accumulate money on a tax-deferred basis is available while valuable life insurance protection is assured at the same time.

An MEC with combination benefits may be an excellent way to transfer wealth to a named beneficiary while preparing for long-term-care contingencies at the same time. It's generally not appropriate, however, if you're younger than 59 1/2, primarily because any withdrawals are subject to a 10 percent early withdrawal penalty similar to a traditional IRA withdrawal. In other words, it's a long-haul investment.

As with buying an ordinary life insurance policy, always shop around for the best deal. Don't look only at dollars and cents either—it's also important to consider the reputation of a company and its longevity.

Accelerated Death Benefits

If you can't afford to over-fund a life insurance policy in the form of a modified endowment contract, perhaps that ordinary life insurance policy you took out years ago, or even an affordable new policy, could be the gold mine you need as a contingency against catastrophic illness. Some existing policies allow for the addition of a long-term-care rider in the form of accelerated death benefits. With the rider, if you need long-term care before you die, you can tap the policy benefit—typically 2 to 4 percent of the death benefit paid out per month. That will reduce the policy's payout to the beneficiaries after your death, but it's a way to cover your expenses and provide peace of mind while you're alive. If you can't possibly envision yourself ever needing long-term-care insurance, but still want to make a few contingency plans just in case, this may be the option for you.

Let's assume, for example, that your plain-vanilla life insurance policy has an accelerated death-benefit rider. And let's suppose you develop a chronic disease like multiple sclerosis or insulin-dependent diabetes and need long-term care. Instead of struggling to pay for your care as your heirs wait for you to die to get any financial relief, you can access a portion of the death benefit of your life insurance policy—perhaps 25 percent up to 50 percent—while you're alive, to help pay those costs.

This kind of living benefit can be a valuable financial planning tool. Long-term-care insurance will cost more and its benefits may be better, but the accelerated death benefit allows your money to do something for you while you're alive. Because you're able to tap only a portion of the benefit, though, it may not provide as much money as a modified endowment contract with combination benefits—but then, it didn't cost as much up front either.

Events that typically trigger benefits in a life insurance policy with accelerated benefits (compared with a life insurance policy with a true LTC rider) include terminal illness or permanent confinement to a nursing home.

Life Settlement

If you develop a chronic illness, don't overlook life insurance policies as a solid source of immediate cash—that equity infusion you need to pay for care expenses in the form of a life settlement.

A life settlement involves selling an unwanted or unnecessary life insurance policy to a third party for more than its surrender value and less than its net death benefit (the amount paid out at death, less any debts due on the policy). The seller receives immediate cash for the policy from the purchaser. The purchaser, if it's a third party, in turn becomes the new beneficiary of the policy and is responsible for all premium payments from the time of purchase until the seller dies, at which time the third party receives the death benefit amount.

Keep in mind that if your life insurance policy has a long-term-care rider, allows you to convert it to that, or if you can qualify for and afford a new policy with the rider, selling the policy generally may not be the best option for you.

When to Consider a Life Settlement

- *If you don't need a life insurance policy anymore, it's an alternative to stopping your premiums and getting nothing.*

- *If your life insurance policy premiums are too expensive.*

- *Medical/long-term care is needed.*

- *Interested in charitable/family gifting.*

- *Change in employment status.*

- *Bankruptcy as a means of paying off debt.*

- *If you're older, in poor health, and need money to pay current living expenses.*

- *Your policy is about to lapse.*

Life settlements aren't as widely used or as mainstream as some other financial tools. Nonetheless, they generate an estimated $240 million annually to those people who sell their policies, according to *The Benefits of a Secondary Market for Life Insurance* by Neil A. Doherty and Hal J. Singer, a study from The Wharton Financial Institutions Center, Wharton School of Business, University of Pennsylvania.

A life settlement can be an excellent, and often untapped and overlooked way of turning an illiquid asset into a liquid one in your lifetime. A similar type of life insurance resale known as *viatical settlements* surfaced in the 1990s as a way for AIDS sufferers and other terminally ill people to help pay for their care. Viaticals were based on the assumption that the original policyholder was expected to live only a short time. In those early years, the little-regulated industry ran into widespread fraud. Today the environment is better regulated. It's important to note that some states and/or organizations mean different things by the terms *viatical* and *life settlement*, so be sure you know all the details.

For a person to qualify as "terminally" ill, a physician must certify that he or she has less than 24 months to live. A "chronic" illness requires a physician to certify a person's inability to perform two of any six of the activities of daily living (the ADLs we talked about earlier).

The National Association of Insurance commissioners has defined guidelines to avoid fraud, and organizations such as the Life Insurance Settlement Association and the Life Settlement Institute have been established to uphold industry ethics. The association's members must comply with ethical standards and be fully licensed to do business in the life settlement industry. The institute works to raise awareness of the industry.

How it Works

Let's look a little more closely at how a life settlement works. A transaction generally involves four major players:

- **Policy seller:** Usually seniors older than 65 with a life expectancy of more than two years and up to 10 years with a recent change in health that's resulted in higher life insurance premiums.

- **Financial advisors:** Before selling any policy, involve your financial advisors, such as a CPA, elder-law attorney, financial planner, or estate planner. Usually they're more familiar with life settlements and can help you make informed decisions that work best for your situation.

- **Brokers:** A financial advisor can do the transaction for you, but in an industry where the market values of life insurance policies are private, someone with the ability to deal with multiple advisors can net more money for you, the seller. (To find a qualified broker near you, visit the LISA Website, *www.lisassociation.org*.)

- **Providers:** The entity that pays the policy holder a cash sum for his or her policy.

For example, if an individual has a policy for $100,000, he or she might be able to sell that policy for $10,000, $15,000, or even $20,000. Depending on the seller's age, state of health, policy, and cost of premiums, he or she could sell the policy for as much as $50,000. If the seller has a $1 million policy, he or she might sell it for perhaps $100,000 to $150,000, or, if in very ill health, perhaps as much as $500,000.

More Details

A few other issues to keep in mind if you're thinking about a life settlement:

- The money you receive in exchange for your policy is tax-free up to the amount of the premiums you've paid in. Any tax liability on the remainder depends on a number of factors, so always check with your tax advisor *before* you sign on the dotted line.
- Policy restrictions may apply. For example, usually a policy must be valued at $100,000 and up.
- If you sell your policy, your heirs lose any of its death benefits.

Getting the Best Deal

If you're still interested, always shop around for the right buyer. That means, try to get three offers and compare them. Who is willing to give you the most money for your policy?

Make sure you're dealing with a completely reputable and well-known broker or agency. These kinds of settlements are an excellent tool when done correctly. If they're not, they can create heartache and pain—often at a time when someone already is stressed and under duress. Again, always talk to your financial advisor as well as family members *before* ever signing on the dotted line for this transaction. Also, check the background of the buyer to make sure it's a sound company. You can do that through your state's insurance commissioner or department (links available at Advantage Compendium: *www.indexannuity.org/states.htm*). It's generally a good idea to work with big-name carriers to simplify the process and avoid headaches.

Roadmap to Success

Beyond the Medicaid/forced poverty route, you have options to fund your long-term-care needs. They include long-term-care insurance, a modified endowment contract with life and long-term-care benefits, accelerated death benefit, life settlement, or variations/combinations of these.

No matter your age, take the time to explore what works best for you and your loved ones. There is no one-size-fits-all; everyone's situation is unique. And don't automatically assume you can't get, can't afford, or can't qualify for what you need. You don't know for sure unless you try. Remember the morbidity versus mortality issue? Long-term-care insurance looks at your likelihood of getting sick, and life insurance considers your mortality—the likelihood of death.

Whatever you decide, though, make sure the company has a solid reputation, a good track record, and will be around when you need it, especially if that's likely to be some time far in the future. Check on any potential insurance provider before you sign anything. Start with your state's insurance department or commissioner to learn if any complaints have been filed against the company, and check out its rating with any of the various rating agencies.

When looking for the solution that's right for you, pay attention to your potential longevity. If most people in your family live to age 90, look for a long-term-care funding solution that will cover you way down the road if you need it, as opposed to a short-term answer.

More Resources

- Covenant Consumer Resource Center (*www .covenantresource.com*): A consumer-oriented Website from Matt Rettick and his Covenant Reliance Producers team dedicated to helping preretirees and retirees access the necessary information to safeguard their estates and become financially fit for life; check out the free booklets available on a variety of topics.

- Bankinsurance.com (*www.bankinsurance .com*): Great links to all kinds of organizations, regulators, and more to do with banking, insurance, and securities.

- Life and Health Insurance Foundation for Education (*www.life-line.org*): A nonprofit organization with lots of free information on life, health, disability, and long-term-care insurance; includes glossaries and free consumer guides; check out its "Find an Agent" link from its home page.

- Life Insurance Settlement Association (*www.lisassociation.org*): Nonprofit that promotes the development, integrity, and reputation of the life settlement industry; includes answers to questions on life settlements as well as links to state requirements (click on "Settlement Req.").

- LTC Consultants (*www.ltcconsultants.com*): From nationally recognized long-term-care authority and consultant Phyllis Shelton (author of *Long-Term Care: Your Financial Planning Guide*, LTCi Publishing, 2007). Click on "Consumer Information" to access valuable and helpful information.

Chapter 8

Step 5: Annuities—The Path

to Retirement Security

The best way to double your money quickly is to fold it in half and put it in your pocket.

—Matt Rettick

As traditional pension plans—those with defined benefits— go the way of the dinosaur, the retirement landscape is changing dramatically for most Americans. No longer is income stream in retirement a guarantee. In today's era of defined contribution plans—401(k)s and the like—your retirement savings are up to you. If you don't save, invest, and make the right choices with your retirement and potential retirement monies, you're out of luck!

We have all heard or seen the news reports about the retirees and soon-to-be retirees who lost their life savings as major U.S. companies like WorldCom, Tyco, and Enron hit bottom. Many of those people chose not to diversify their holdings in their 401(k) plans, and that, combined with the apparent corruptness of their employers, spelled their doom.

Even if you get part of investing or money-managing right, your entire financial future—except for what may or may not be Social Security down the road—is at the mercy of someone else. The 401(k) plan manager, your personal money manager, a mutual fund manager, or someone else, is in charge. That person or persons must make choices about, among other things:

- The right moves to make with your savings based on current trends that change daily.
- The right time to buy a seemingly attractive investment.
- How much to buy.
- When to sell.
- How much to sell.
- What to do with the money after the sale, and so on.

And, of course, the markets, the world situation, governments, and interest rates all need to cooperate too. In other words, if you put all your retirement savings in a 401(k), the deck is stacked against you before you start. You may be putting your money—your future income in retirement—at risk.

401-KEG: A New Retirement Option

Here's some hypothetical calorie-free food for thought when it comes to investing:

- *If you purchased $1,000 in Nortel (NYSE: NT) stock at the beginning of 2001, nine months later your investment would have been worth about $137. Nortel shares went from $36.16 cents a share on January 4 that year to $4.98 a share on September 21.*

- *If you had bought $1,000 of Enron on December 28, 2000, and sold it November 28, 2001, your investment would be worth just $11.66.*

- *With WorldCom, if you bought the $1,000 worth in July 2000, and sold it in December, the value of your original investment would have dropped to about $286.*

- *If you purchased $1,000 worth of beer a year ago, drank the beer (or dumped it on the lawn as fertilizer), then turned in the cans for recycling, you could have $214 for your efforts.*

But you can hedge your bets, bypass these variables, and come up with a viable financial solution that will pay you a regular income stream in retirement and ensure that your money won't run out before you die. Most likely, you'll have money left over for your heirs too. In some cases, if you choose, you can even capitalize on the gains of the equities markets without the risk of losing your principal or your annual gains.

We're talking about annuities—specifically, fixed annuities and fixed indexed annuities (formerly called equity indexed annuities). Other than Social Security and a defined pension benefit plan (assuming either doesn't run into financial trouble), annuities are the only way to absolutely guarantee that your money won't run out before you do. And if you don't have or don't expect to have any kind of a company pension, a fixed annuity plan that pays a regular monthly income stream makes a great deal of sense.

We'll talk more about specifics later. But first, let's look at annuities in general.

What Is an Annuity?

An annuity is a contract—most often with an insurance company—that calls for a lump sum investment or investments through time for a specific period. Earnings on the principal grow tax deferred and are due only at the time of withdrawal or payout. At the time of the owner's death, any balance that hasn't been withdrawn is paid out to the annuitant's beneficiary either in a lump sum or through time.

> *The annuity concept dates back to the Roman Empire!*
>
> *—The 2004 Annuity Fact Book*

Annuities aren't new. In fact, they've been around for literally thousands of years. At the time of the Roman Empire, contracts known as *annua* promised a series of payments for a set length of time or for a single payment. A form of annuity also was popular in Europe in the 17th, 18th, and 19th centuries.

Today's annuities can be fixed or variable. With a fixed annuity, the interest rate the account earns is specified in the initial contract. Generally, annuities pay a fair rate of return, although not the very highest. But, in exchange, your principal is protected from the ups and downs of the markets because your earnings are ironclad guaranteed, period. Consider that if you deposited $100 in a fixed indexed annuity, it continues to grow and earn and compound without market risk to that principal, and with stock market–linked gains locked in no matter how wildly markets seesaw. Fixed annuities also offer no front-end loads (fees) and no commission charges to a client, as well as a guaranteed death benefit and the opportunity to convert this accumulating asset into an income stream you cannot outlive.

A variable annuity, on the other hand, offers the chance of greater returns, but at a price. Your money—your investment—is at risk. You can choose various options of funds in which to invest your annuity. Some even have fixed-return options too. But the rate of return and the value of your principal fluctuate depending on the performance of the investment. Typically these annuities offer a guaranteed minimum death benefit to the annuitant, or owner of the annuity. However, the cash value available to you could be significantly less than the death benefit if the market declined substantially.

With an immediate annuity, the annuity purchaser pays a lump sum, and in turn immediately begins receiving a monthly income stream. That income stream continues for a specified number of years, or a lifetime. The amount of those withdrawals depends, obviously, on the amount of the single premium, as well as the length of time of the annuity.

Annuitization provides the only viable way to achieve a secure lifetime income without spending substantially more money. In fact, achieving the same level of security for lifetime income will cost 25 to 40 percent more if you put that money in typical investments such as stocks and bonds. And even *that* won't guarantee you won't outlive your money because of changing interest rates, according to David F. Babbel, professor of insurance and finance at the University of Pennsylvania's Wharton School of Business. Babbel and Craig B. Merrill, professor of finance and insurance at The Marriott School of Management at Brigham Young University, both fellows at Wharton Financial Institutions Center, examined investing and retirement in their study, *Rational Decumulation*, co-sponsored by Wharton Financial Institutions Center and New York Life Insurance Company.

"People worry about markups on annuities, but our studies found that how much you pay relative to what you get has gone way down in recent years," says Babbel:

> *Think of stock mutual funds where you pay, on average, 1 percent to 2 percent every year to manage your money plus 5 percent to 8 percent more as an up-front or back-end load in many cases. Over time these percentages accumulate to a hefty chunk of your investment, according to several recent studies. Annuities may take just 3 percent. In other words, price*

competitiveness has reduced the markup on these annuities to basically close to nothing.

Sensible and Sound

Last year, Americans sank more than $236 billion into annuities, with about $75 billion of that in fixed annuities, according to LIMRA International, a worldwide association that provides research, consulting, and other services to nearly 850 insurance and financial services companies worldwide (*www.limra.com*).

About $25 billion was spent on fixed indexed annuities, according to Advantage Compendium (*www.indexannuity .org*). A good chunk of those investors were retirees. The reason: retirees recognize the value and security of this excellent retirement account. Typically these fixed indexed annuities peg their returns to popular market indices such as the S&P 500, Dow Jones Industrial Average, NASDAQ, S&P 400 Mid-Cap, or Lehman Brothers Bond Index.

Benefits of a Fixed Annuity

- *Safety of principal.*

- *Liquidity.*

- *Good, competitive returns without risk.*

- *Preferential tax treatment [Section 72 of the IRS tax code (Annuities; Certain Proceeds of Endowment and Life Insurance Contracts), which sets taxation rules for payouts from annuities].*

- *Avoids probate if beneficiary named.*

- *No IRS Form 1099 to file unless interest is withdrawn.*

- *No stock market risk.*

- *Can provide a regular income you can't outlive.*

- *Flexible, exchangeable through a 1035 exchange (a tax-free exchange under section 1035 of the IRS Code). See www.irs.gov/irb/2003-33_IRB/ar11.html.*

- *No front-end fees or annual charges.*

- *May avoid nursing-home spend-down.*

- *Incontestable on death of annuitant.*

- *Can provide a structured payout to heirs or beneficiaries.*

- *Economic depression protection.*

Betsy and Bill both retired at age 65 at the height of the stock market's Internet craze, when seemingly every technology stock was a goldmine. All their friends were raking in the cash from their equities investments, so the couple decided to invest $100,000 in the market. That first year their investment climbed 50 percent. Betsy and Bill were thrilled. The second year, it climbed another 50 percent and the couple began planning their life of leisure, figuring there was no end in sight. That third year, though, their portfolio lost 50 percent. Undaunted, they blamed the paper loss on the whims of the tech world, but still figured that they had increased the value of their investment significantly if they sold their stock because their account had climbed as high as $225,000. Right?

Wrong! Actually the account would be worth only $112,500. (That's the $100,000 initial investment, which grew to $150,000, and then $225,000, before losing 50 percent of its value, leaving the $112,500.)

If, instead of jumping onto the Internet bandwagon, they had put their $100,000 in a fixed indexed annuity (more details later), they wouldn't have had the heady gains, but they would have come out much further ahead. Let's say that the first year the indexed annuity earned 50 percent of the actual market gain (that's 25 percent), the second year another 25 percent, and the third year the market tanked, down 50 percent. It doesn't matter to Betsy and Bill. Their savings are in a fixed savings vehicle. The account now would be worth more than $156,000, and those gains are tax-deferred until withdrawal! The couple takes a little bit less upside gain with the indexed annuity in exchange for incurring *none* of the downside risk. If they chose their annuity right and it carries the provision that locks in annual gains, if the market went down another 25 percent the next year, the couple's portfolio still would be worth more than $156,000.

Legal Reserve Requirements

Worried about the safety of your money with an insurance company? Don't be. Buying an annuity through a reputable insurer comes with legal, government, and industry protections.

First, for every dollar you invest in fixed annuities, the insurer by law must set aside more than $1 as a guarantee to handle claims and various expenses. That's known as the legal reserve.

In most states, insurers also must participate in a guarantee fund pool to protect policyholders in case an insurer goes out of business. If that happens, the other insurers step in and take over so that all policyholders are protected. Insurers also are licensed and regulated by the state insurance commission in the state where they operate. A number of rating services keep tabs on the strength of various insurance companies and their operations too.

Still worried about the safety of your money if it's held by an insurer? Consider a few facts about the insurance industry:

- During the Great Depression, the insurance industry bailed out the banking industry.
- The life insurance industry controls more assets than all the world's oil companies combined.
- The life insurance industry also has more assets than all the assets in the world's banks combined.
- The life insurance industry doesn't lend out your money to others as banks do.

When it comes to retirement, you can worry about plenty more pressing and riskier choices than annuities.

Fixed Indexed Annuities

A fixed indexed annuity is an annuity that carries a fixed minimum interest rate of return and ties the possibility of additional gains to a popular equities index such as the S&P 500. For example, depending on how gains are credited to your particular annuity, if the S&P 500 goes up 10 percent in one year, you could gain all or a part of that 10 percent increase. If it goes down, you lose Z-E-R-O. Your earnings are flat for that year, but your principal and previous gains are locked in. You lose nothing. It's all about the power of zero.

Remember Ann, the mom who wanted to ski with her kids, so she tried the LaLanne course to fitness? After getting physically fit, she decided to shape up financially for her future as well, and bought a $100,000 fixed indexed annuity. The first year the index went down. How much of the $100,000 did Ann lose? ZERO. The second year, the index went up 12 percent, and Ann's annuity gained 10 percent, the maximum allowed under her annuity, so that she now had $110,000. The next year, the index fell again, but not the value of Ann's account. Her loss: ZERO, and she still retained her $110,000 that included the monetary gains of the previous year. The up-and-down cycles continue, with

Ann's annual gains locked in and protected from loss during the down years.

Even with a crystal ball, we can't accurately predict markets year to year. But with a fixed indexed annuity, you don't have to. You're protected. You can sleep at night without worrying about your money. When the index you've chosen goes up, you lock in your gains, and when it goes down, you don't lose a dime. Apparently a lot of people have gotten wise to indexed annuities: In the last 13 years, more than $130 billion in fixed indexed annuities have gone into effect!

Fixed indexed annuities are simple to understand, but made complicated by insurance companies.

—Jack Marrion, Advantage Compendium

Overcoming the Confusion

The variety of fixed indexed annuities on the market may seem dizzyingly complicated and confusing. More than 50 insurance companies offer different variations. But don't panic. The variations merely are different ways companies use to figure interest gains.

2006 Top 10 Producers of Fixed Indexed Annuities (By Sales)		
Rank	Company	Total sales (in $millions)
1	Allianz Life	$6,681.4
2	Aviva	2,537.4
3	ING	2,303.2
4	Old Mutual	2,079.6
5	Midland National Life	2,003.1
6	American Equity	1,787.2
7	Equitrust	1,001.3
8	Jackson National Life	947.8
9	Jefferson-Pilot	871.8
10	Sun Life	731.1

> Source: *Advantage Index Sales and Market Report,
> 2006; AnnuitySpecs.com*

Medicaid-Friendly Fixed Annuities

An annuity is the only savings/investment vehicle that can change from an asset into an income stream, and that's critical when it comes to Medicaid planning. Not all fixed annuities, however, are Medicaid-friendly under current laws (those laws could change). Currently, to qualify, an annuity must:

- Adapt to Medicaid regulations, including one specifying that the money paid back by the annuity throughout the life expectancy of the annuitant, or purchaser, must be equal to or greater than the initial deposit that went into the annuity.

- Be actuarially sound, according to the Centers for Medicare and Medicaid Services' tables. That means the number of years of guaranteed payout must be within the annuitant's life expectancy, according to specific numbers as outlined by the government in what's known as "HCFA Transmittal No. 64" (check it out from third-party Medicaid Planning Systems LLC, *www.medicaidplanningsystem.com*).

- Be able to annuitize—the asset can become an income stream that's paid out over time.

- Specifically allow a change of ownership if necessary.

If your money is in a Medicaid-friendly deferred annuity and you have to enter a nursing home, the annuity is simply annuitized—it becomes a guaranteed income stream almost like a pension plan, and, instead of being counted as an asset, it's considered income. The income also must go to the at-home spouse, who is allowed unlimited income.

Unfortunately, the options are limited for single people. Because there's no "at-home spouse" to receive the income, a single person can give away assets (with qualifications we'll talk about later) or annuitize those assets to be paid out to themselves throughout their life expectancy in accordance with specific life-expectancy tables. The monthly income then would go to the nursing home for cost of care, and Medicaid would make up the difference for the total cost of care. Basically, this kind of an annuity delays the inevitable dependence on Medicaid.

Maria, 70, and never married, needed nursing-home care. She had $100,000 in assets that she used to purchase a Medicaid-friendly immediate annuity, which would pay her a monthly income stream. Because, according to government tables, at age 70 she had a life expectancy of 14.3 more years, the annuity paid her approximately $600 a month, spread out over the next 168 months (14.3 years). That's $100,000, divided by 168 months, or $600 a month. Her monthly care cost amounted to $4,000, so Maria paid $600 of it, and Medicaid picked up the remaining $3,400.

One catch, however, thanks to the Deficit Reduction Act of 2005: Because the income is payable to Maria, the institutionalized person, the state is the remainder beneficiary. It gets what's left if Maria doesn't exhaust the money in her annuity before she dies. If she outlives the annuity, Medicaid will end up footing the entire bill. (More on Medicaid in Chapter 10.) Don't let yourself be overwhelmed by all these details. It's not as complicated as it sounds, and a qualified financial advisor can help you with the different ins and outs.

Remember Andrew from Chapter 1? His wife had Alzheimer's and was in a nursing home that cost Andrew $6,000 a month out of pocket for her care alone. The solution to the crippling drain on Andrew's limited finances was a qualified Medicaid annuity. He also then set up a revocable living trust (it included his other assets and the house) in case he died before his institutionalized wife did. In essence, by setting up the trust and funding it with his assets, Andrew disinherited his wife. That sounds a bit cruel at first, but look more closely. By doing so, the assets would pass to his heirs instead of to his wife. If instead she were to receive that asset or income, her Medicaid eligibility would be revoked and the money would be eaten up by the cost of her care. If that happened, she would be right back where she started, with Medicaid footing the bills and her children left with nothing!

By buying the annuity with a lump-sum payment from their savings and setting up the trust, both parents are protected from outliving their money, and their hard-earned assets, if any are left, are assured of going to their offspring, the beneficiaries/heirs of the trust that contains the annuity. Andrew, with the help of his seasoned financial advisor, had prepared for the "what ifs" of the future.

> *Always think about and make contingency plans for the future.*
>
> *—Matt Rettick*

Not long after he'd set up the annuity and trust, Andrew unexpectedly contracted cancer. When he died a year later—his wife was still in the nursing home—his kids were amazed at their inheritance. They'd assumed that all their parents' assets had been depleted by their mom's long-term-care costs.

Tax Advantages

When Andrew's children received their inheritance, very little income tax was due on it. The reason: The money primarily was principal, not interest, and therefore not a tax liability.

Whether an annuity is fixed, as in Andrew's case, or variable, its earnings are federal and state income tax-deferred until withdrawn. The earnings do not count toward their income threshold for the purposes of Social Security tax either. This triple tax exemption adds to the value of compounding to build interest on your savings. You earn money on:

- Your principal.
- The interest gains.
- That amount of cash that normally would have been paid in taxes each year.

Henry and Katherine purchased a $200,000 fixed annuity at 5 percent for 10 years. That means their investment will earn 5 percent every year with earnings from interest locked in every year whether interest rates go up or down, markets go up or down, or the country is at war or peace.

Avoid Probate

Probate is the legal process involved in verifying that a will is valid and legal. The will must go before the court for this verification before assets may be distributed. The process can take anywhere from a couple of months to several years and even longer, and can involve costly legal fees. An annuity with a named beneficiary, however, bypasses probate and is distributed directly to the beneficiary. When Andrew died of cancer, for example, his children were named as beneficiaries of the annuity. The money went directly and almost immediately to them on proof of his death; they simply provided a notarized copy of the death certificate. The annuity was exempt from the probate process. The money, of course, was still part of his estate for inheritance and estate-tax purposes, but its distribution wasn't delayed or bogged down by the legal system.

Had Henry and Katherine both died before the term of their annuity expired, the annuity also would have passed unencumbered to their niece, the beneficiary as named in the annuity.

Stretch IRA-Friendly Annuities

Annuities can also be advantageous across generations. These are known as *multigenerational IRAs* or *stretch IRA annuities*. When the owner of such an annuity dies, no lump-sum income taxes on earnings are due. The vast majority of the balance can continue to grow because only small minimum annual withdrawals are required and thus potentially subject to taxation. That can make a huge difference in the growth of the annuity.

Let's look at how this works. Ross owned a $100,000 multigenerational IRA. At his death, it automatically passed to his named beneficiary, his 40-year-old daughter, Ellen, without any probate or court delays. Ellen wasn't required to cash in the annuity for the lump sum, and therefore didn't face the potentially decimating tax liability of an ordinary IRA. Instead, she left her dad's IRA in his name, with her as the inherited beneficiary, and planned to let it grow and compound throughout her life expectancy. Each year she was required to take out only minimal amounts—the required minimum distribution.

Cashing in Across Generations

Multigenerational IRAs, or stretch annuities, allow heirs/beneficiaries to receive lifetime income across two generations (children and grandchildren), compared with typical lump-sum distributions that end up decimated by tax liabilities. Consider the following numbers and scenarios:

Initial IRA Amount: $500,000

Earnings: 6 percent interest rate

Gross withdrawals/distribution to initial owner (ages 70-83): $374,079

Ending IRA balance at initial owner's death: $596,622

Typical lump-sum IRA distribution

Starting amount: $596,622

Income taxes due (at 28%): $167,054*

Amount left for heirs: $429,568

Multigenerational IRA or annuity

Starting amount: $596,622

Income taxes due: Varies depending on the age of heir; due only on annual withdrawals/distributions taken by heirs throughout their lifetimes

Gross lifetime withdrawal/distribution**: $2,536,934

*Depends on income tax bracket.

**Includes distributions to, in this case, a son ($1,397,993) and a grandson ($1,138,941) of initial IRA/annuity owner

Source: Covenant Reliance Producers LLC

Richard always wanted to leave a financial legacy for his son Mark, so he bequeathed him a hefty IRA valued at $1 million. That, Richard assumed, would more than ensure the future of his three grandchildren. Unfortunately, Richard neglected to consider the government's role in his estate. On Richard's death, taxes ate up almost two-thirds of the legacy's value. Mark was left with about $357,500 after tax liabilities—35 percent income taxes and 45 percent estate taxes (top tax brackets for 2008).

Conversely, consider what would have happened if Richard had put that $1 million into an approved multigenerational IRA fixed annuity. At the time of Richard's death his son Mark, and Mark's three children, as named beneficiaries of the annuity, immediately would have received the inheritance without the delay of probate, and would not have had to pay *any* income tax on it (the annuity would be subject to estate taxes if the gross estate including the IRA exceeds the federal exemption). Remember that with an annuity, the income tax liability on earnings is deferred until the money is withdrawn. Throughout time, that $1 million easily could grow to $7 to $8 million. Now *that's* the kind of legacy Richard would have wanted for his grandchildren!

Annuities With Long-Term-Care Riders

A fixed annuity with a long-term-care rider just might be the best of both worlds—the growth and security of an annuity, and the peace of mind and security of long-term-care insurance. It's an investment with all the benefits and tax-deferred growth of an annuity, *along with* a provision to ensure payment for care for the long term if it becomes necessary. It's investment and catastrophic-illness planning in one.

Unlike long-term-care insurance, in which you pay out premiums in exchange for what may be a future need, an annuity with a long-term-care rider ensures that your money remains yours and continues to grow. It's there for you if you need it; otherwise the annuity remains your investment.

Before you opt for an annuity with a long-term-care rider instead of a modified endowment contract, long-term-care insurance, or other life insurance investment, however, it's important that you understand fully its pros and cons.

Drawbacks of Annuities

We've discussed the upsides, so now let's consider a few of the downsides too.

- **Taxable gains:** The tax liability of an inherited annuity is based on the difference between the annuity's initial purchase price by its original owner and its current value when you, as heir, sell it. That differs from the step-up basis valuation that applies to tax liabilities on inherited stocks. (Step-up basis pegs the starting valuation at the date of original owner's death.) Ordinary IRA annuities are also fully taxed.

- **Tax rates:** Annuities are taxed at ordinary tax rates (currently 10 percent to 35 percent), and not the generally lower capital-gains rates (currently 15 percent).

- **Government penalties:** Similar to an ordinary IRA, withdrawals from a deferred annuity before age 59 1/2 usually result in a 10 percent IRS penalty, plus the income tax due on the money.

- **Surrender charges:** These are early withdrawal fees that, with exceptions, usually must be paid to an insurer if an annuity is cashed in before the end of its term. It's basically a penalty agreed to up front should you renege on your contractual obligation. Some contracts do allow ongoing withdrawal or withdrawal of small amounts (normally 10 percent per year), free of charges. Traditional deferred annuities, however, generally have surrender fees, but they are reduced or eliminated in time, which can range from five to 20 years. The longer the annuity is held, the less the surrender charge. For example, if you have a $50,000, 10-year annuity contract, and decide to pull out after two years, you will face a penalty fee (a policy's penalties differ), whereas if you pulled out after 10 years, you would have no surrender fees. Annuitants, however, are guaranteed their full money back during the "Free Look Period," which normally is 20 days from receipt of the annuity contract.

- **Limited access to principal:** If you opt for an immediate annuity, one that pays a regular income stream, remember that the principal is not readily accessible should you need money in addition to that lifelong income stream.

- **Variable annuity fees:** Fixed annuities and fixed indexed annuities have no up-front charges. Variable annuities, however, have annual fund expenses. If you opt for a variable annuity, make sure you fully understand all the fees and the reasons for them.

As with any other investment or major purchase, always talk with your financial advisor and thoroughly understand the details and ramifications, short and long term, before signing on the dotted line or putting down any money.

Why Opt for an Annuity?

In general, when it comes to being prepared for future potential long-term-care costs, long-term-care insurance is the best option. But if you can't afford it or can't qualify for it, and you're looking for a savings account in which the safety of your principal is more important than high rates of return, the answer is a fixed annuity.

Keep in mind, too, that if you don't qualify for long-term-care insurance you may not qualify for life insurance either, so, again, a Medicaid-friendly fixed annuity may be your only option to handle future long-term-care costs. It can also be a solution if you truly can't get long-term-care insurance and need an income stream either immediately or down the road.

And, as we talked about earlier, the annuity's unique ability to be converted from an asset into an income stream makes it an ideal financial tool with Medicaid planning in mind.

Ranking the Options for Long-Term-Care Funding

Beginning with the best approach:

1. *Long-term-care insurance with inflation protection.*

2. *Modified endowment contract.*

3. *Life insurance policy with long-term-care rider.*

4. *Annuity with long-term-care benefit.*

5. *Life settlement.*

Source: Covenant Reliance Producers LLC

Roadmap to Success

Most people can't afford to risk the loss of their principal, no matter their age. Among other essentials:

- A properly structured fixed indexed annuity that pegs its gains to a popular market index is an excellent savings vehicle to protect your principal, and provide competitive gains, with low risk to you. When the markets go up, you lock in your gains, and when they go down, you don't lose a dime. It's all about the power of ZERO...as in zero losses!

- After your death, an annuity with a named beneficiary bypasses what can be the cumbersome probate process and is distributed directly to the beneficiary.

- Annuities can be stretch IRA–friendly, and thus have the potential for tremendous growth throughout generations. When the owner of such an annuity dies, no lump-sum income taxes on earnings are due (although the annuity is subject to estate taxes if the gross value of the estate exceeds the allowed exemption). The vast majority of the balance can continue to grow, because only small minimum annual withdrawals are required, and thus potentially subject to taxation.

- Annuities also are available with long-term-care riders.

- Remember that annuities are taxed at income tax rates, not the lower capital-gains tax rates.

- Before buying an annuity, be sure you're aware of any early surrender fees that might be due if you need the money prior to its payout date.

More Resources

- AnnuiWeb (*www.annuiweb.com*): Not licensed to sell life insurance or annuities, the site provides information on annuities and related products; includes an annuity seller locator.

- Covenant Consumer Resource Center (*www.covenantresource.com*): A consumer-oriented Website from Matt Rettick dedicated to helping pre-retirees and retirees access the necessary information to safeguard their estates and become financially fit for life; check out the free booklets available on a variety of topics.

- National Association of Insurance Commissioners (*www.naic.org*): Organization's Website can help you check out insurance companies, link to state insurance regulators, and order free information (click on "Consumers") about annuities.

- Safe Money Places® (*www.safemoneyplaces .com*): A Website that doesn't sell anything but does provide all kinds of helpful information, statistics, and guidance on a variety of ways to invest, with your money's safety in mind.

Chapter 9

Step 6: Investment Management—Maximum Returns With Minimal Taxes, Fees

Proper planning prevents poor performance.

—Matt Rettick

Now that, hopefully, you have a better idea of the importance of your future fiscal fitness and the components that make it possible, let's see how to combine those parts into a money-management platform that works for you. No matter your age, the goal is to take the necessary steps now to ensure that you and your loved ones remain financially secure and fiscally fit today and down the road. As we've discussed, financial fitness includes everything from making sure you have the necessary documentation in place, to buying long-term-care insurance, seriously considering fixed indexed annuities or other options that provide guaranteed income for life, buying life insurance with your loved ones' financial future in mind, and more.

Fiscal fitness also involves knowing how to manage your other assets—your investment portfolio—wisely.

Maximum Returns

In other words, you must learn how to invest your nest egg for maximum return with minimal risk—and pay the lowest taxes and fees allowed by law.

If you're already retired and living on a fixed income, you may prefer the safety and security of fixed indexed annuities that don't risk your principal in the stock market.

But what about your other assets? With inflation running at about 3 percent, stashing cash under the mattress is not a viable option. Interest on a money market account probably won't cover—let alone beat—inflation for the long haul either.

Or what if you're not retired and are actively looking to grow your nest egg? How can you generate double-digit returns on investments with fiscal fitness in mind?

In this age of low interest rates and returns, making your money work hard for you is a tall order, especially without taking big risks. But with the right approach, guidance, and direction, it is possible to combine financial gain and fiscal security. No matter our age, income, or personal and financial goals, we all would all like to make maximum return on our money while paying minimal taxes and fees. But how is that possible without risking the hard-earned principal we've discussed throughout this book?

The answer is a sound money-management platform that includes carefully considered investments. We're not suddenly advocating that you toss financial caution and moderation to the wind, or that you forget the long-term-care insurance, fixed indexed annuity, life insurance, and other essentials so you can invest in frivolous stocks. We are by no means talking about bingeing on high-flying investments or the financial fad of the month. We *are* suggesting that you—with the help of your financial advisor—take a big-picture, long-term look at what you have. After you account for funding your long-term care, life and other insurance policies, as well as an annuity, then you can take systematic steps to maximize returns on your remaining investment dollars.

To get an idea of the strategies needed to navigate the convoluted world of investments, we talked with Dean Zayed, JD, LLM, CFP®, and CEO of Wheaton, Illinois–based Brookstone Capital Management, LLC. He's a top-notch investment advisor with a tried-and-true approach that blends risk, return, and tax savings. All that adds up to fiscal fitness with your future in mind.

Let's look more closely at how some of Dean's ideas on money management can be integrated into our approach to fiscal fitness.

But first things first!

The Importance of Finding the Right Financial Advisor

Many advice books deal with investment approaches initially and financial advisors later. That's the cart-before-the-horse approach. You need to find the right financial advisor up-front, and then together the two of you can chart your personal course to fiscal fitness.

Why Bother With an Advisor?

An advisor can help make your financial life hassle-free and secure. This isn't a realm for do-it-yourselfers. Too much is at stake. After all, we're talking about your future and that of your loved ones. What if you forget a crucial detail? What if you miscalculate, or your figures are off? What if you overlook a deadline, a signature, a rollover? Given any of these scenarios, you very well could end up outliving your money! And then what happens? Will you be reduced to relying on Medicaid? We'll talk about that in Chapter 11.

With the right advisor, however, those considerations become moot.

What should you expect from a good advisor? As Zayed says:

> *I talk with clients at length, meet with them to better understand who they are, and I have them fill out a lengthy questionnaire so I can understand their unique situation and best define their financial profile. That way, I can tailor a solid money-management platform that truly meets their needs, wants, desires, and goals both today and in the future. You should expect the same from your own advisor so he or she can build a customized money-management platform for you that is suitable, provides a comprehensive solution, and is a direct match to your financial profile that your advisor has helped you define.*

If you work with the right professional, he or she undoubtedly will bring up issues you're unaware of and interject essential discipline and guidance into your fiscal strategy. A truly professional advisor takes emotion out of the equation so you can make the right moves at the right times to meet and exceed your needs and goals.

"In my years as a financial planner," says Zayed, "the one thing I have found that clients overlook the most often—the biggest mistake they make—is failing to take a truly long-term view of their financial picture. By long term, I mean visualizing their financial picture 25 to 35 years *after* retirement, and maybe even longer.

"With today's life spans and lifestyles," he adds, "those numbers are reality. We need to recognize that and deal with it. The alternative is to outlive your money, and none of us wants to face that."

But, you say, "I don't need a financial advisor. I don't have that much money or that many assets to worry about."

Whatever you think of your financial situation, you can't afford *not* to talk to an advisor. Everyone should sit down with an advisor at least once to see if it's worth pursuing a more ongoing relationship. One visit is a small price to pay, and the rewards can be huge.

"After all," says Zayed, "you've spent your entire life accumulating assets. Regardless of their amount, don't you think it's worth an hour of your time to sit down with a professional to see if there are money-management steps you can take today to plan for your long-term-care needs and retirement, and to help ensure that you don't outlive your money? Your family's interests are at stake too."

Whether your assets total $100,000 or $10 million, at some point it makes sense to have an objective professional take a look at your situation and offer his or her educated advice.

Selecting a Knowledgeable Advisor

These days it seems as if we're constantly bombarded with investment advice or the marketing to promote it. Whether via the mailbox, telephone solicitations, television and radio ads, e-mail, or some other venue, everyone has the "perfect" way to invest your hard-earned dollars.

How can these hard marketers have the right plan for you and your needs without even knowing you? That's the point. They can't, and they don't! Forget those advertisements and marketing ploys. The most important consideration in finding a potential financial advisor is a personal referral, period. Everyone knows someone—friend, family, business associate, or whomever—who has had a successful relationship with a financial advisor. If you want someone to paint your house, check the Yellow Pages. If you want an advisor to help chart your fiscal future, look for personal referrals.

> *Personal referrals are the No. 1 way to find the financial advisor who is right for you.*
>
> —Matt Rettick

Don't overlook your other advisors either, as sources for a referral. That reputable agent you've worked with and trust for long-term-care or life insurance also may have the expertise and credentials to advise you, or may be associated with an organization that can provide top financial guidance and direction. For example, my company, Covenant Reliance Advisors, is dedicated to helping its network of financial advisors provide the best possible guidance and direction for their clients. I'm licensed to sell insurance, and, similar to Dean Zayed, I'm an investment advisor representative through Brookstone Capital Management. Brookstone is an Illinois investment advisory firm registered with the Securities and Exchange Commission.

Beyond personal referrals, a couple of other places that may help you get started in your search for an advisor are:

- Financial Planning Association (*www.fpanet.org*): Offers a free search tool to help you find Certified Financial Planner professionals.

- The American College (*www.theamericancollege .edu*): The Bryn Mawr, Pennsylvania–based nonprofit educational institution has provided professional education to raise the standards of the financial services industry since 1927; includes all kinds of helpful information and resources for consumers and financial professionals; check out its "Find an Advisor" link.

No matter where you find potential advisors' names—even if through a referral from a friend—be careful. Thoroughly check out any individual's or organization's qualifications and credentials. Ask for references too, and check each one. Some other good places to check up on an advisor include:

- Securities and Exchange Commission (*www.sec .gov*): Click on "Investor Information," and then "Check Out Brokers & Advisers."
- FINRA, formerly NASD (*www.finra.org*): Click on "FINRA BrokerCheck."
- BBBOnline (*www.bbbonline*), or your local Better Business Bureau.

The Issue of Compensation

When looking for an advisor, it's also important to consider how he or she earns his or her paycheck. Payment options include:

- Commission: a certain percentage or amount of cash earned for the products sold.
- Flat fee: per hour or a set amount for handling or providing a certain service.
- Fee-based percentage: The amount could vary depending on the amount invested and the performance of the portfolio.
- Combination of fee-based and commission.

The fee-based approach offers certain advantages when it comes to dispensing financial advice. The better your investments perform, the greater your advisor's compensation. That's incentive for both of you. Another advantage of this and other fee-based systems is that no hidden costs or fees are lurking. With this arrangement, all fees are fully disclosed and therefore transparent. You know up-front what you will pay for what advice and direction.

That doesn't necessarily mean you should rule out advisors who earn commissions, however. In fact, many advisors earn commissions on certain products, and charge fees for other services.

"I think the most flexible approach to compensation is for an advisor to be both fee-based and commission-based because that allows the advisor to offer you, the investor, access to the entire universe of investment options and vehicles with no limitations," says Zayed.

Shea, 63, and her husband, Bart, 68, relied on the advice of Liam, a financial advisor Shea had consulted before the couple was married 30 years earlier.

"Liam has been a longtime family friend. Back then and still today I trust his advice implicitly," says Shea. "He's helped us generate a nice nest egg. He earns his money through a combination of fees and commissions, which, of course, he discloses clearly up-front. I would recommend him to anyone."

Jack, on the other hand, prefers working with an advisor strictly on a fee basis. "Why would I want anyone whose own interests don't align with my own? The bigger my portfolio, the bigger my advisor's paycheck," he says.

Whichever you prefer is fine, as long as you know and understand up-front how your particular advisor is to be compensated. How do you discover that? ASK!

More Questions for Potential Advisors

Beyond the compensation structure, talk to potential advisors about their investment approach and how they work with clients. Do they work unilaterally, or do they allow client input? During your initial meeting, pay attention to whether the potential advisor is paying attention to *you*. Or is he just telling you what he does and how he operates and how you should go about it? Remember, as we've said, each of us has a different financial profile with different needs, approaches, risk tolerances, and so on. You want your advisor to tailor your money-management platform to you, and not some idealized cookie-cutter method that is generic in nature.

And, of course, do you *like* the person across the table? Do you think you can develop a long-term relationship with that person? Both of those questions require a yes if you want your money-management platform to succeed.

Lastly, does your potential advisor answer your questions willingly and thoroughly? This is your money and you must understand what's happening with it.

Keep in mind too that if you choose a particular advisor and aren't satisfied with his or her performance, you are free to move on. Find another advisor. That's your right and privilege, and you've earned it.

Asset Allocation

The most important concept in putting together a money-management platform to meet or exceed your needs and goals today and tomorrow is asset allocation. *Asset allocation* is investing or allocating a set amount or percentage of your assets—from cash to IRAs to 401(k)s—in different types of investments with different levels of risk and return. In doing so, you create a kind of insurance policy against the ups and downs in industries, companies, and markets at any given time. This kind of diversity provides essential protection for your portfolio.

Forget about investing for a moment and consider what would happen to your corner grocery if it carried only one product or only one brand of drink or cereal. How would that affect its business, and, as a result, its finances? Or what about a hardware store that sells snow shovels only and nothing else year 'round? That store might sell bundles of shovels in the winter, but what would happen to its business during the summer?

Chances are that neither retailer would last very long. Of course, these are ridiculous scenarios. Retailers must diversify product lines as insurance to draw customers and sell products no matter the weather or the various tastes of potential customers. It's the same with your investment portfolio. You gain security through diversification of assets—the right mix in the right investments.

Remember Arnie, the 62-year-old widower who woke up to physical fitness the LaLanne way and then decided to get fiscally fit too? Arnie bought his long-term-care insurance policy and then talked to his financial advisor. Together the two of them took stock of Arnie's assets. Arnie wanted to put almost everything except his house into a fixed-indexed annuity. That way, he figured, he would avoid risking his money in the market and not have to worry again. His advisor, on the other hand—because of Arnie's age, newfound health, and the fact that he had excess cash—suggested that Arnie put a percentage of his money into the annuity, and then allocate the remaining portion into a properly asset-allocated, diversified portfolio with a suitable amount of risk, per Arnie's risk tolerance level. Such a portfolio would provide Arnie additional possibilities for greater investment growth and higher returns. He would benefit in the short run, and his heirs would gain in the long run. Arnie liked the idea, especially because he was considering some world travel, which might affect his near-term financial needs.

Remember Betsy and Bill from Chapter 8, the couple who wanted to get in on the high-tech craze and invested $100,000 in technology stocks? Because the couple didn't diversify their investments, their savings—and would-be nest egg—were subject to the unpredictable whims of technology at a time when Internet stocks were on a wild roller-coaster ride. When the Internet bubble burst, the couple's nest egg exploded. If, instead, they had worked with a qualified financial advisor and allocated their assets according to their present and future needs, wants, and goals, the collapse in technology markets probably would have had far less effect on their portfolio.

Profiling That Counts

How you allocate your investment dollars depends on you and your individual situation, which is known as your *financial profile*. Everyone has his or her own unique profile based on age; income; financial, physical, and health needs; goals now and in the future; tolerance for risk; dreams for you and your loved ones; and so on. As we've talked about, your profile—similar to your health—is never static. It's constantly changing. Once Arnie recovered his physical health, his fiscal needs changed too. Instead of worrying strictly about a roof over his head, food, and clothing, he began to entertain ideas of traveling the world. That meant his future financial needs—his financial profile—changed.

René, 63, was divorced, and had two grown children, and three grandchildren. Both of her kids were single—one a confirmed bachelor, the other a financially struggling single mom of three. Since René's ex-husband long ago had dumped the kids, she constantly worried about making sure all her grandchildren had money for college.

René was comfortable financially and for years had worked with a top financial advisor, so her investment ducks were in a row to cover the grandkids' education. Or so she thought. Her bachelor son fell in love, married, and he and his new wife had twins! Now the grand-brood had grown to five, and suddenly it wasn't quite so simple to cover all their future college expenses. René's family profile had changed dramatically, and as a result, so had her fiscal profile. She and her advisor headed back to the financial drawing board. Now instead of three Section 529 plans in place—one for each of the grandkids—she has five. These plans, named after the Section of the IRS Code that establishes them, enable earnings inside an account to grow tax-free. The distributions are tax-free too, if used for a qualified higher education expense. (Check out *www.savingforcollege.com* as a resource to compare various 529 options). René also, with the advice of her advisor, has her contributions to these accounts automatically withdrawn from her checking account so that she contributes regularly. In doing so, René is *dollar cost averaging* her investment as opposed to trying to *time the market*—picking the right time every time to invest for maximum gain. Doing the latter consistently is tough. Even the smartest brains on Wall Street can't successfully time the market consistently.

As with René's situation, different data points make up your financial profile. In order for an asset allocation program to work for you, it must align with your unique data and situation.

Elements of Your Asset Profile

All of the following and more combine to form your financial profile:

Age

Income

Health

Personal goals

Financial aspirations

Family issues

Estate concerns

Managing for Maximum Returns and Minimal Taxes and Fees

You literally have tens of thousands of options for investing your money, ranging from single companies to investment pools, such as mutual funds, to pieces of real property, or real estate investment trusts (REITS), to notes of credit, such as certificates of deposit, and much, much more. Investment vehicles are prolific too, ranging from individual investments to retirement accounts, savings accounts, and beyond. We can't touch on each one, but we can provide a brief overview of the general approach we like when it comes to ensuring your fiscal fitness with maximum returns, and minimal taxes and fees.

"I subscribe to the core-and-satellite approach to asset allocation," says Zayed. "Done right, it means minimal risks, maximum gains, with minimal taxes and fees, keeping in mind that every client's portfolio must match the risk tolerance."

With this approach, your portfolio is composed of a foundation, or core component that represents 50 to 70 percent of your assets. These assets are invested in the highest quality, most stable companies that pay high dividends and whose stock generally is held for the longer term. These companies most often are Dow Jones Industrial Average stocks. They're the Wal-Marts of the world, so you won't find any start-ups, fleeting fads, or rocky sectors here.

The other 30 to 50 percent of the portfolio is made up of satellite components—companies or funds across the investment spectrum that provide above-average returns and add value to the portfolio. This portion of the portfolio is much more active. Holdings are bought and sold for maximum gains for minimal periods. These holdings could include small-cap funds, or funds or stocks specific to various trend sectors such as energy, real estate, or technology.

Minimize Your Tax Bite, Fees

Buying and selling lots of stocks or funds typically means paying lots of fees and incurring lots of tax liability—or does it? If you combine actively managed mutual funds with passively managed index or exchange-traded funds, you *can* lower your costs and fees.

Mutual funds raise money from the sale of fractional shares of their portfolio of assets, and are run by professional fund managers who invest those assets according to the fund's stated objective. That objective could be income or growth, or could be based on an industry or sector, such as telecommunications or energy, or even based on a geographic area, such as Japan or Asia. Because the fund manager's day-in and day-out work is to make the most of your money, the fund generally comes with higher fees, or loads. Mutual funds also regularly distribute capital gains or losses that could result in annual tax liabilities for you.

Index or exchange-traded funds are not actively managed, and therefore have much lower annual management fees. An index fund is a mutual fund made up of stocks in a specific index, so it tracks an index such as the Standard and Poor's 500 or Dow Jones Industrial Average. An exchange-traded fund, or ETF, also mirrors an index such as the S&P 500, but has certain trading specifications and is therefore not considered a mutual fund. Popular ETFs include Barclay's I-shares, SPDRs (Standard and Poor's Depositary Receipts), and Vanguard's ETFs.

ETFs are low cost and generally—but not always—more tax efficient than many mutual funds because they're not actively managed and therefore usually have less turnover in their portfolio holdings. Turnover, which is when a security is bought or sold, results in capital gains or losses that are passed on to investors and end up creating a tax liability for the investor. Be sure to talk to your advisor and select an ETF carefully, because some can have high turnover (high capital gains tax liabilities), just the way some mutual funds can have low turnover (low capital gains tax liabilities). Check out the free online Expense Analyzer from FINRA, the nongovernmental regulatory organization created in July 2007 with the consolidation of NASD and the member regulation, enforcement, and arbitration functions of the New York Stock Exchange *www.finra.org/ InvestorInformation/InvestmentChoices/MutualFunds/ index.htm*).

Other characteristics of ETFs include:

- Continuous trading/pricing throughout the trading day as opposed to mutual funds that are priced at the beginning and end of each trading day.
- No additional internal cost for transactions unlike many mutual funds. ETFs do have to pay for the cost of a trade, however, but those costs are often offset by lower annual fees.
- The average ETF expense ratio is about 0.5 percent lower than that of a mutual fund.

Why Bother With Mutual Funds?

Exchange-traded funds are a great addition to your portfolio. But for maximum portfolio growth, you still need to include mutual funds. It's that diversification factor again. ETFs are designed to mirror a market or an index. Mutual funds, on the other hand, can outperform it, and in turn increase your chances for potentially stellar returns. Combining active and passive money-management vehicles has proven to yield better long-term results akin to what the large institutions do. It's as simple as that.

But that doesn't mean all mutual funds have equal advantages. As with ETFs, select carefully.

With Taxes in Mind...

With tax advantages in mind, here are a few other investment vehicle options.

Tax-advantaged retirement accounts. One obvious way to minimize your tax bite is to maximize contributions to tax-advantaged retirement accounts such as 401(k)s and IRAs. Such contributions often are tax deductible, with their earnings and growth tax-deferred. Take advantage of any matching funds programs through employers, too. That's free money that also grows tax-deferred. Even if your employer doesn't provide matching funds or you don't qualify for tax deductions for contributions to IRAs, your earnings still grow tax-deferred.

Bonds. Bonds, especially broadly diversified bond funds, play an essential role in the stability of any portfolio. Bond funds can be made up of perhaps 200 *different* bonds so that the default of any one bond doesn't impact the overall portfolio. Bond funds can also expose an investor to every segment of the bond market, from mortgage-backed to corporate, government, high-yield, and more.

Five Portfolios For Different Investment Goals

Brookstone Capital Management suggests several different models of asset allocation with different goals in a portfolio:

Current Income:

- *The primary objective is to provide risk-adjusted returns slightly above the yield of a relatively risk-free 10-year Treasury bond while minimizing the loss of principal. This strategy includes a diversified mix of assets that includes a majority exposure to short and intermediate high-quality fixed-income assets, with the remaining allocation to U.S. large-cap equity and unit investment trusts (UITs).*

Growth and Income:

- *The primary objective is to provide risk-adjusted returns between the long-term expected return of a diversified high-quality bond portfolio and that of a broad stock market index portfolio, with a level of total risk closer to a diversified bond portfolio. This strategy includes a diversified mix of bonds and stocks, with emphasis on the highest-quality-rated intermediate sector of the bond market, and a majority exposure to high-quality fixed-income assets, with the remaining allocation to global equities, including U.S. large-, mid-, and small-cap equity, as well as developed international and unit investment trusts (UITs).*

Conservative Growth:

- *The primary objective is to provide risk-adjusted returns near the expected return for the total U.S. stock market, with the potential for slightly less downside risk as opposed to the total stock market. This strategy includes allocations to bonds and equities with a slight emphasis on a diversified mix of global equities, including allocations to the U.S. large-, mid-, and small-cap equity and developed international markets.*

Moderate Growth:

- *The primary objective is to provide risk-adjusted returns slightly above the expected return for the total U.S. stock market, with the potential for slightly less volatility than a 100 percent S&P 500 Index-like portfolio. This strategy includes a diversified mix of bonds and stocks, with emphasis on a diversified global stock portfolio. The fixed-income portion focuses*

*on high-quality U.S. bonds, while the equity alloca-
tions include U.S. large-, mid-, and small-cap equity markets, as well as developed international and
emerging markets.*

Growth:

- *The primary objective of this strategy is to provide
  risk-adjusted returns above the expected return for
  the total U.S. stock market, with the potential for
  equal or slightly higher risk than a 100 percent diversified U.S. equity portfolio. This strategy includes
  a diversified mix of global equities, including allocations to U.S. large-, mid-, and small-cap equity
  markets, as well as developed international and
  emerging markets.*

Source: Brookstone Capital Management
(www.brookstonecm.com)

Pay Attention to Fund Managers

When choosing an investment strategy, don't focus too
much on any individual fund company. Instead, pay attention to its fund manager and his or her track record—
throughout 10 years, if possible. After all, a fund's performance
is not based on the name of its parent company; it's up to
the investment prowess of its manager. If he or she can
read the market and understand the big picture and its nu-
ances, he or she will make the right moves, and the fund
will perform well. If a manager isn't attuned to the market,
the fund will show less than projected growth.

"I don't care what company a particular fund manager
works for–Vanguard, Oppenheimer, Strong, Merrill Lynch,
on and on," says Zayed. "I follow the manager."

The Medicaid Catch

For soon-to-be retirees trying to grow their nest egg but facing the very real specter of nursing-home confinement, investing is still an option. Of course, if done well, the right investments could mean you no longer need to worry about spending down or giving away assets so you can qualify for Medicaid to pick up the cost of your long-term care.

But if you simply don't have enough money to invest, or your current needs don't give your money time to grow, you must work with your advisor to put together a plan for gifting and spending down those assets that must go. It's far better to do it your way than to lose it all to Uncle Sam.

Again, all these issues are part of the financial profile that a reputable financial planner can help you outline. Based on that profile, the two of you then can determine your fiscal fitness plan.

Revisit Constantly

Just as your financial profile isn't static, neither is your financial plan. It's a dynamic process that evolves through time with changes in your life, your goals, your health, and with market conditions too. Concerning the latter, for example, a couple of years ago a real estate investment trust (a pool of real estate investments) and mortgage-backed securities were excellent investments with good growth potential. But that was before the real estate downturn, and before the shakeout in the subprime mortgage markets.

Remember René and Arnie, and how their lives and lifestyles changed? Yours undoubtedly will change too, so it's vital to revisit your financial plan once a year. That's especially important as you grow older and face the possibility of long-term-care needs.

Tune out Hollywood and the Hype

One last piece of investment advice: Forget the investment chatter out there as Hollywood meets Wall Street. Tune out those broadcast media types—television, radio, and Internet—who hype you up and leave you hanging with the latest, and what they consider the greatest, in investment advice. The Jim Cramers of the world are selling TV ratings and aren't genuinely interested in your investing future. You can't afford to listen to what they say. Just know that whatever they say is in their *own* best interests. Remember, it's your savings, your future, and the financial future of your loved ones that are on the line.

If you have to read, click, listen, or watch, do so as entertainment, not as a substitute for the personalized, educated advice of your financial professional. Stick with a financial advisor you like, trust, and who is going to provide a course of action and discipline tailored for your fiscal fitness. He or she should be your financial quarterback. Pay attention to the advice, and your portfolio will score.

Roadmap to Success

- Fiscal fitness involves knowing how to manage your investments wisely with the help of the right financial advisor.

- The best source to find a financial advisor is a personal reference. That perfect advisor for you may even be that reputable agent you know and trust who sold you that long-term-care insurance policy, life insurance policy, or fixed indexed annuity.

- Having an advisor is important, because he or she becomes the objective, third-party quarterback of your assets and investments, who can help you make the right decisions for your future.

- The most important concept in creating a money-management platform to meet and exceed your needs and goals is asset allocation. That's spreading or diversifying your assets among various types of investments with varying risks and returns. It's an insurance policy of sorts for your portfolio.
- The right kind of core and satellite approach to asset allocation will generate maximum returns with minimal taxes and fees.
- Index funds that track stock indices and exchange traded funds (ETFs) can be tax-efficient ways to generate solid financial gains.
- Visit with your financial advisor at least once a year to update your asset profile and adjust your portfolio to meet the needs of that new profile.

More Resources

- BBBOnline (*www.bbbonline.com*): As an online version of the Better Business Bureau, it's a great place to check out any complaints against a potential financial advisor.
- Brookstone Capital Management (*www.brookstonecm.com*): A Wheaton, Illinois–registered investment advisor that currently serves clients across the country.
- Covenant Consumer Resource Center (*www.covenantresource.com*): A consumer-oriented Website from Matt Rettick dedicated to helping pre-retirees and retirees access the necessary information to safeguard their estates and become financially fit for life; check out the free booklets available on a variety of topics.

- FINRA (*www.finra.org*): This is the primary private-sector regulator of America's securities industry and oversees activities of brokerage firms and registered securities representatives. Check out free potential brokers with its BrokerCheck, or mutual funds and ETFs with the Fund Expense Analyzer, and visit its comprehensive Market Data Center for answers to all kinds of investing and savings questions.

- Securities and Exchange Commission (*www.sec.gov*). Government organization, offers plenty of investor and consumer information and is a good source to check out a potential investment advisor or broker.

Chapter 10

Step 7: Tap Your Home's Equity—You've Earned It!

Dead equity is like dead calories. It's no good for you.

—*Matt Rettick*

Equity is all about value and ownership. When talking about a house or condo, equity is the value of the property that belongs to you, minus any mortgage due on the home. When referring to an investment, equity is that portion or share that's yours. Don't be afraid of your equity in anything. It is, after all, yours. You've worked for it; you've earned it. It's your money, your asset, your equity.

A big part of becoming fiscally fit is to understand what your equity—as in your home—can do to help you, and then how to make the right choices so that it works *hard* for you. Ideally, you want to make the most of your equity while keeping the safety and security of yourself and your loved ones in mind.

A reverse mortgage, available to those homeowners age 62 and above, can accomplish just that, especially when it comes to preserving affordable quality of life and remaining in your own home as long as possible.

Why Consider a Reverse Mortgage?

We've all heard it dozens of times: Probably the largest purchase any of us will ever make is our home. Most people work a lifetime, tap their savings, borrow huge sums, and pay tens of thousands of dollars in interest for the privilege of home ownership. It is, after all, a huge part of the American dream. In fact, 81 percent of householders age 65 and older in 2006 owned their own home (U.S. Census; *www.census.gov/hhes/www/housing/hvs/hvs.html*).

Because owning that home has taken so much effort to achieve, why not let that home make life easier for you in your retirement? A reverse mortgage can provide cash to help fix up your house or fund your care if you're chronically or even catastrophically ill. It can give you the wherewithal to remain in your home for your lifetime instead of being forced into a nursing home. Conversely, it can pay for nursing-home costs, thus allowing you to avoid dependence on Medicaid and keep you in control of your life.

A reverse mortgage is a nonrecourse loan—you don't have to qualify and you don't have to repay the money during your lifetime. It's available to those age 62 and older who live in and own their home. Even if your home isn't paid off, you could be eligible for a reverse mortgage. Remember, it's based on your equity—your ownership share. You or your spouse can't be kicked out of your home, either, even after the term of the mortgage runs out.

A reverse mortgage is for life. It has no term, so not matter how long you or your spouse live in your home, there will be no requirement to repay the reverse mortgage as long as taxes and insurance remain current.

—Monte Howard

The money you're eligible to receive is based on the appraised value of your home, the amount of income you desire, and your age (generally, the older you are, the more money available to you). You can take the money in a lump sum, as a line of credit, or paid out over time—monthly as income, perhaps—and use it for whatever you like, from vacation homes to home repairs to home healthcare. Better yet, use the money for an annuity or to pay long-term-care premiums.

The mortgage company can sell the home after your death (or, for married couples, after the death of the second spouse), or after you move out. If the home sells for more than the money paid out, the remainder goes to your chosen beneficiaries. Or, you or your heirs can sell the home, repay the reverse mortgage, and then keep what's left.

Common Misconceptions

- *A reverse mortgage means that the bank takes your house after the mortgage term ends.* Incorrect! You and your spouse continue to own the home and are the only names on the deed or title. Reverse mortgages are designed to tap only a portion of your equity, so you may be able to pass on an inheritance or have money left over from the sale of your home should you decide to move.

- *Reverse mortgages are only for desperate seniors or for those who are "house rich, cash poor."* Incorrect! This type of loan is used by homeowners from all walks of life to enhance their retirement years. The growing popularity of this product highlights its benefit to help homeowners deal with many different financial situations.

- *You must be debt-free to qualify for a reverse mortgage.* Incorrect! Even seniors with an existing *mortgage on their home and other debts may qualify. The reverse mortgage can eliminate the need to continue to make monthly payments on that debt, freeing up valuable cash on a monthly basis.*

- **When a reverse mortgage comes due, the bank sells the home.** *Incorrect! When the loan must be repaid, you or your heirs can either pay the balance due on the reverse mortgage and keep the home, or sell the home and use the proceeds to pay off the reverse mortgage. You or your heirs keep the money left over from the sale of the home, above and beyond the reverse mortgage balance.*

Source: Use Your Home to Stay at Home™: Expanding the Use of Reverse Mortgages to Pay for Long-Term Care, *The National Council on Aging, study funded by the Centers for Medicare and Medicaid Services and Robert Wood Johnson Foundation*

Who's Doing It?

If it's so great, why isn't everyone taking out a reverse mortgage? First, reverse mortgages haven't been around that long. They only began to take off in the early 1990s. But a public awareness campaign combined with skyrocketing long-term-care costs have finally begun to awaken the public to the value that home equity can have when it comes to aging and care. In fiscal year 2000, there were just 6,600 home equity conversion mortgages (HECM), the federally insured reverse mortgage product. By fiscal 2005, that number had climbed to 43,000; in fiscal 2006 it soared to 76,000, with that number expected to near 90,000 in 2007, according to testimony by Brian D. Montgomery, assistant secretary for housing, U.S. Department of Housing and Urban Development, at a hearing before the Senate Special Committee on Aging, February 15, 2007.

(*www.fha.gov/press/2007-02-15testimony.cfm*). HECMs account for the vast majority of all reverse mortgages made in the United States. Most of the rest are through private lenders.

But that's just a drop in the bucket as far as the potential for reverse mortgages to help Americans plan fiscally for their future. Even the federal government is considering ways that home equity and reverse mortgages can help solve the healthcare funding dilemma faced these days by so many Americans as they age.

The nonprofit National Council on Aging estimates that more than 13 million Americans literally are sitting on almost $700 million in potential reverse mortgages that could help with the cost of their care-giving and long-term care. That's according to a study entitled "Use Your Home to Stay at Home™: Expanding the Use of Reverse Mortgages to Pay for Long-Term Care," released by NCOA, and funded by the Centers for Medicare and Medicaid Services, the federal agency that operates Medicare and Medicaid, and the Robert Wood Johnson Foundation.

As part of the *Use Your Home to Stay at Home*™ project, a variety of free brochures and materials about reverse mortgages (*www.ncoa.org*) are available for consumers. NCOA estimates that of the more than 13 million Americans who are good candidates for reverse mortgages, each household on average would be eligible for $72,128! That's no small chunk of change.

The nonprofit National Council on Aging (www.ncoa.org) *offers free brochures to consumers as part of its Use Your Home to Stay at Home™ project. The U.S. Department of Housing and Urban Development (http://www.hud.gov) is another good source of information on reverse mortgages, as is the National Reverse Mortgage Lenders Association* (www.nrmla.org).

Dead Equity

Remember when we talked about physical fitness and nutrition, and the importance of eating foods loaded with vitamins and minerals as opposed to those with empty calories? That natural, fresh vegetable salad, for example, is far better for your health than that chocolate bar loaded with little more than dead calories.

Well, when the equity in your home is not being used to make your life a whole lot easier, it's similar to empty, worthless calories. A paid-off or nearly paid-off mortgage is an asset that's not earning interest, not providing any benefit, not working for you. It's not even keeping ahead of inflation. And, if you're retiree age, that equity could be the answer to your financial needs.

It's that simple. A reverse mortgage can create a regular stream of income to enable you to remain in your home and to afford the cost of long-term care, in-home assistance, and/or medical care. But you have to take advantage of this opportunity you've earned, this opportunity you've worked so long to achieve.

As we've mentioned, if you take out a reverse mortgage, neither you nor your spouse can be turned out of your house as long as you keep the taxes and insurance current— even if the term of the reverse mortgage ends. And after you've moved on or died and the house is sold to pay off the reverse mortgage, your heirs cash in if the sale generates money in excess of the cost of the reverse mortgage!

Art and Cynthia, both in their early 80s, were in relatively good health but had slowed considerably and needed help. Their children were flailing about for a solution because they couldn't be there every day to provide the assistance their parents required.

The couple had no real savings and relied on Social Security and a modest pension. They also had no long-term-care insurance, or any other long-term-care plan. The only option for Art and Cynthia, their children assumed, was to file for Medicaid and move into a nursing home. But Art and Cynthia stubbornly refused to do that. They had lived in the same home for 45 years, raised their two children there, and simply did not want to move, especially because a move might force the couple to split up. Their solution: a reverse mortgage, taking a nonliquid asset—their house—and turning it into a liquid one—cash, in the form of a reverse mortgage. Their house, which was paid off, needed a new roof and a couple of upgrades to meet minimum standards, but the money from the reverse mortgage easily could pay for those repairs, and then the couple could still draw a regular income for the rest of their lives. Their home, their castle, became their lifeline. The extra money could provide funds to pay for a regular homemaker aide and occasional home healthcare. The couple could stay home, stay happy, and stay together.

At first Art and Cynthia worried that by tapping their home's equity, they were taking away their children's inheritance. But the home, after all, was the result of the 45 years Art had spent working hard as a bricklayer. The couple decided that it indeed was theirs to use for their needs.

When Does a Reverse Mortgage Make Sense?

The National Council on Aging's *Use Your Home to Stay at Home™: A Planning Guide for Older Consumers* suggests a few situations in which reverse mortgages work well for seniors. In all three instances, the home is valued at $150,000.

Lou, 75, needed home repairs (just as Art and Cynthia did) and homemaker help to remain in his home. He received a lump sum of $90,120 from his reverse mortgage, out of which he paid $10,000 for home repairs, and then kept the rest in a line of credit to pay for extra in-home help as needed, and to buy new tires for his car.

Janet, 85, has arthritis, and requires extra help from a neighbor, whom she pays $1,000 a month. She also sometimes needs a home-health aide, which can boost her monthly bill for help to more than $3,000. She opted to take out a reverse mortgage in the form of a line of credit for $106,754. At current interest rates, that will cover monthly expenses of $1,000 for more than 12 years, or $3,000 a month for more than three years.

Tom and Jill Smith, ages 69 and 65, have long-term-care insurance that will be there when and if they eventually need it. But right now they want to add a bathroom to their home's first floor to cut down on climbing the stairs. Based on Jill's age, the Andersons receive $74,798 from their reverse mortgage. Out of that money, they can add the bathroom, and then keep the rest to meet any additional expenses.

Drawbacks and Concerns

Reverse mortgages aren't for everyone. As with any other financial planning tool, it's important to look at the advantages and disadvantages as well as your own unique situation to determine if a reverse mortgage is right for you or a loved one.

For example, a home might not meet minimum building standards and require too much investment to make a reverse mortgage worthwhile. The repairs, in other words, would eat up the entire home's equity. In Art and Cynthia's case, as well as Lou's situation, their home repairs were minor enough and their home's value great enough that the reverse mortgage left plenty of equity and value for their future living expenses.

Also, some progeny stubbornly refuse to condone their aging parents' taking out a reverse mortgage, claiming that the family home is *their* inheritance. As selfish and cruel as that sounds, it's more common than you might think. In a situation such as that, a parent or parents could bring in outside experts to help the children recognize the importance of the situation. A qualified financial advisor can also help parents work with their children to understand the situation and the alternatives, as well as provide the parents with support for their decision.

If neither you nor a loved one plans to remain in the home for very long, the cost of the loan may not make economic sense. Those costs can add up to more than 5 percent of the home's value, according to The National Council on Aging numbers, so it may not be a fiscally sound decision in some cases.

The Details

Reverse mortgages are available from a variety of banks and private lenders as well as through the federal government. It can pay to shop around, including checking out the Federal Housing Authority (FHA)-insured Home Equity Conversion Mortgage from the U.S. Department of Housing and Urban Development (*www.hud.gov*). That's one of the most popular options, and can often be the one with the lowest costs.

Reverse mortgages aren't only for those with low-value homes, either. Fannie Mae (*www.fanniemae.com*) has a Home Keeper® reverse mortgage with a $417,000 limit as of 2007, and Mountain States Mortgage Centers (*www .mountainstatesmortgage.com*) offers reverse mortgages and traditional mortgage solutions, as well as a useful consumer Website.

Home Equity Loan

Homeowners who are adamantly opposed to a reverse mortgage or who don't know how long they realistically will remain in their home may want to consider a conventional home equity loan as an option to generate cash instead. The loan can be in the form of a home equity line of credit, which can be used for whatever the homeowner wants, with no restrictions.

A home equity loan, however, can be a costly solution for the short term because the homeowner must make minimum monthly interest payments. It can make sense if the interest rate on the loan is low and the homeowner doesn't plan to remain in the home for long. Plus, a home equity loan keeps home ownership intact. At the homeowner's death, the home remains a legacy to pass to heirs, minus the outstanding balance on the home equity loan.

Keep in mind, though, that a homeowner must qualify for a home equity loan. That means he or she must be able to meet the monthly payments or risk losing the home.

Roadmap to Success

Don't be afraid to use the equity in your home that you've built up with time. You've earned it. That's what a reverse mortgage is all about. Even if you or your spouse are not yet 62—and therefore ineligible for a reverse mortgage— you may want to think about it as a future option to pay premiums for long-term-care insurance, or even a lump sum to fund a modified endowment contract or other form of long-term-care contingency planning.

If you already qualify for a reverse mortgage and are considering it, keep in mind that neither you nor your spouse can be kicked out of your home, even if the term on your reverse mortgage expires.

You can take payment from your reverse mortgage in a variety of ways, ranging from a lump sum to a line of credit or monthly payments. In other words, it can create a regular stream of income to enable you to remain in your home and to afford the cost of long-term, in-home assistance and medical care.

Your home, however, *does* have to meet certain building standards to qualify for a reverse mortgage, but you can pay for those upgrades from proceeds from your reverse mortgage. But it may not make sense if your home's value is such that the cost of improvements leaves little cash left over for your needs.

More Resources

- AARP (*www.aarp.org*): The nonprofit organization is a gold mine of information on all kinds of senior and aging topics; type "reverse mortgage" into its search engine.

- Mountain States Mortgage Centers (*www .mountainstatesmortgage.com*): Composed of reverse mortgage lenders that offer reverse mortgages and traditional mortgage solutions; the Website includes general helpful information and questions/answers for consumers.

- National Center for Home Equity Conversion (*www.reverse.org*): Includes some helpful information and explanations on reverse mortgages.

- ReverseMortgage.org (*www.reversemortgage .org*): From the National Reverse Mortgage Lenders Association, an industry organization, the site offers consumer information, guidance, and free resources (including brochures) on reverse mortgages and more; click on "Locate a Lender" to find a reverse mortgage lender in your state.

Chapter 11

Step 8: VA Benefits and Medicaid

> *Medicaid may be a last resort, but with proper planning you can safely protect your assets from disappearing.*
>
> —*Matt Rettick*

Attention, veterans and spouses of veterans—and we're not referring only to career military or military retirees, either. You may be eligible for significant benefits, financial and otherwise, as you age. Sure, Uncle Sam has education programs and benefits that you may or may not be eligible for, and, after you die, you probably can get a free burial in a national cemetery. But wouldn't an extra $20,000 a year make a big difference in your ability to afford the care you need in the event of chronic, catastrophic, or terminal illness? The answer to that question probably is a resounding yes.

Without those benefits or advance planning, your primary alternative could be Medicaid. That's the state-administered, federal/state-funded program of financial assistance for medical care for the poor. As we've mentioned, when it comes to nursing-home care, Medicaid picks up the cost of almost half of the nation's more than 1.8 million nursing-home residents. In other words, all those Medicaid recipients are poverty-stricken.

Sound fishy? It's not. Most of those people didn't start out poor, but became that way in order to qualify for financial assistance from the government. They either planned ahead to spend down enough to become eligible for Medicaid, or they were forced into it if they wanted to become eligible by default. Whether you or your loved ones are financially well off, comfortable, or have only enough to get by, you'll have to get rid of your assets (with a few exceptions we'll discuss later) if you expect to get Medicaid relief, without penalty, from the crippling cost of long-term care in a nursing home. With certain exceptions, Medicaid generally doesn't pay for assisted living or home healthcare.

Let's look more closely at the options.

Help for Veterans

As a veteran—there are an estimated 9 million age 65 and older (U.S. Census, 2005 Community Survey; see *www.census.gov/Press-Release/www/releases/archives/ facts_for_features_special_editions/009715.html*)—a regular income stream could be available to you or your spouse now or even after your death as financial reimbursement for out-of-pocket medical and care expenses if you qualify. The programs are called Aid and Attendance and Housebound benefits, and those who qualify can receive tax-free:

- Up to $1,801 a month for a veteran with a dependent spouse.
- Up to $1,519 a month for a single veteran.
- Up to $976 a month for a surviving spouse of a veteran.

Those maximums also increase annually in line with Social Security increases.

Qualifications include the following four criteria:

1. Served in the military for a minimum of 90 days and at least one day during a declared wartime period (it doesn't matter if you served in the United States or in a war zone). You also must have been honorably discharged.

2. Have a nonservice-related medical necessity that requires a certain level of care or outside help. This includes varying levels of required care ranging from in-home homemaker services to home healthcare and assisted living.

3. Financial need. Your unreimbursed medical expenses must be greater than your total household income (which includes Social Security, pension, interest income, and more).

4. Your total resources cannot exceed more than $80,000 in liquid assets, not including your home. (However, certain conditions apply here as well.)

Legitimate Benefits!

Although many veterans aren't aware of them, these VA benefits aren't a pipedream that no one can qualify for. The money has been appropriated, and if you're a qualified veteran, you've earned it. A qualified veteran can continue to receive the benefits after he or she is in a nursing home as long as he or she is a private-pay patient. If Medicaid foots the bills, however, the Aid and Attendance checks stop.

After the qualified veteran dies, if his or her surviving spouse meets the other requirements (as in financial and physical need), he or she also may be eligible to receive the Aid and Attendance Benefits. In fact, he or she may be able to receive the benefits even if the deceased, qualified veteran never applied for or received the benefits while alive.

There is one catch, however: The Veterans Administration doesn't broadcast the existence of these benefits. In fact, some workers at the VA even deny their existence: But these benefits do exist—and they're probably the best-kept secret in healthcare today! They're mentioned briefly on the VA benefits Website (*www.vba.va.gov/bln/21/pension/vetpen.htm#7*).

If you have your doubts, just ask Maryanne about it. She's an 82-year-old widow of a World War II veteran, a grandmother of three, and a soon-to-be great-grandmother. Until recently she struggled with how in the world to afford the in-home healthcare she needed without asking for charity and without burdening those she loved. That's when one of her grown grandchildren stumbled onto these little-known benefits for veterans.

It was difficult and time-consuming to get all the details of the program, and more than one VA worker told Maryanne they had never heard of such benefits. But after 10 months of dawdling by the VA, Maryanne received her first check in the mail to the tune of $9,200! Yes, the VA drags its feet, but if an application is approved, the VA pays retroactively to the month after the application was made.

The monthly benefit of just less than $1,000 will enable Maryanne to be secure and get the level of help she needs. She's also comfortable in the knowledge that when the time comes, she'll have a guaranteed income—however small—to help with assisted-living costs.

For more information on this program, visit the government's Website (*www.vba.va.gov/bln/21/pension/vetpen.htm#7*) and talk to your qualified financial professional.

Other Options

A variety of other programs and healthcare benefits are available to many veterans. Qualifications for various programs vary, so it's important to do your research, and also check with a VA benefits specialist to make sure you or a loved one receives all due entitlements. Again, these aren't only for career soldiers or military retirees!

- Many veterans are eligible for low-cost prescription drugs available from their local VA hospital. Co-pays often are just a few dollars.
- Qualified veterans may receive free burial in a national cemetery.
- The VA also has nursing homes that provide veterans with care free of charge. However, the waiting lists usually are quite long.

Whatever way you decide to fund your future care needs, don't overlook benefits—such as those available to military veterans—that truly are your entitlements. You worked for those benefits, no matter how long ago that might have been. You built up the equity so that the benefits are there for you when you need them.

In Pursuit of Medicaid

If you're counting on Medicaid to pay for your long-term-care costs, think again. The Deficit Reduction Act of 2005 can mean major out-of-pocket expenses before Medicaid benefits ever kick in, and that's IF you can qualify for Medicaid.

—Matt Rettick

If you're not a veteran, you may, similar to many Americans, look to Medicaid to pick up the cost of your care, provided, of course, that you qualify from a financial standpoint. That often means you'll have to spend down assets to meet Medicaid eligibility rules. You can give away your assets or transfer them to your kids, but either scenario involves very specific steps that require planning far in advance because of newly revised rules for eligibility. Those revisions are part of the Deficit Reduction Act of 2005, which was signed into law on February 8, 2006. This law allows states to "look back" at five years of someone's finances from the date they *file for* Medicaid to make sure they didn't get rid of assets solely to qualify for the "free" care. (Not all states have yet formally adopted or implemented the new federal rules, so check with your local Medicaid office). Previous rules pegged the look-back period at only three years, and from the date an asset was *given away*. That meant far fewer people faced penalties in the form of added out-of-pocket expenses before Medicaid coverage began.

Looking forward under the new rules, if you gave away assets anytime in the past five years or less from the date you *file* for Medicaid eligibility, you'll face hefty expenses for care before Medicaid ever picks up the tab. (Any asset transfer that occurred prior to the new rules taking effect, falls under the old asset-transfer rules, including the three-year look-back). Adding to the hardship, by law, a person can't file for Medicaid until he or she needs it, so, by definition, a person must already be destitute in order to file. They can apply after confinement, but may be turned down. So how will they ever fund their care? Read on.

"The Congressional Budget Office estimates that moving the start of the penalty period from the date of the *asset transfer* to the date of the *application for* Medicaid would result in an average delay of 3 months for Medicaid eligibility for 130,000 by 2015, or 15 percent of new Medicaid nursing home beneficiaries annually." ("Deficit Reduction Act of 2005: Implications for Medicaid," #7465, The Henry J. Kaiser Family Foundation, February 2006).

Of course, if you've made the right kind of catastrophic-illness planning moves— including physical fitness and long-term-care insurance or other options we've discussed—you won't need to worry about losing everything, or about the government taking over your life.

Unfortunately, though, few financial advisors truly understand the Medicaid spend-down process and the techniques and strategies that can prevent someone's life savings from disappearing virtually overnight. Those tactics are ever-changing too. The newest changes as a result of the Deficit Reduction Act of 2005 are just one example of how planning strategies must keep current with changes in the law. And stay tuned: Some of the Medicaid-related provisions of the DRA of 2005 have been challenged in court, so the rules could change yet again. The timetable for states to adopt the new rule varies as well.

Let's take a closer look at what happens when the government weighs in on your future.

Government Intervention

If you're forced to file for Medicaid to finance your care, you'll first have to go through a Financial Resource Assessment. Basically, the Department of Human Services will survey all the assets and income held by you and your spouse. They'll ask for five years' worth of tax returns, investments, savings statements, wills, property deeds, and more. The assets of both spouses are pooled, regardless of whether this is a second or third marriage for either of you, and if you both have prenuptial agreements. Prenuptials are useless when it comes to the spend-down analysis.

Truth Is Stranger Than Fiction

Until recently, giving away assets to qualify for Medicaid was a criminal offense with penalties of up to five years in jail and fines of up to $25,000! It was *known as the 'Granny Goes to Jail Law.' Thankfully, that's no longer the case.*

Certain assets are excluded from the spend-down rules. These are known as *noncountable* or *inaccessible assets*. An individual entering a nursing home is allowed to keep one car, a home if its value is less than $500,000 (some states allow $750,000 in equity; the equity limitation does not apply if a Medicaid applicant has a spouse, child under 21, or blind or permanently disabled child residing in the home), a wedding ring, burial plot, prepaid funeral plan, and around $1,500 of cash value in a life insurance plan. The rest is considered countable assets.

Next, in most states, you must divide all the countable assets in half. The at-home spouse is allowed to keep only half of those assets—up to a maximum $104,400 in cash or investments in 2008 (the amount is adjusted upward annually for inflation). Those assets are called the Community Spousal Resource Allowance and are protected under the Spousal Impoverishment Act of 1988. The institutionalized spouse, however, can retain only $2,000 in assets in his or her name. That means that if your estate is valued at $500,000 (not including the value of your home), you'll have to get rid of or spend down almost $400,000 before Medicaid will pay for your spouse's care.

Remember Andrew in Chapter 1, the 72-year-old whose wife had Alzheimer's and was in a nursing home to the tune of $6,000 a month in out-of-pocket expenses? Before Andrew's Medicaid planning got on track, the couple had about $200,000 in assets plus their car and primary residence as well as a second residence, which was the family's 200-year-old homestead (not an excluded and allowable asset under Medicaid rules). What if Andrew had tried to qualify his wife for Medicaid without the right kind of planning? Not only would he have had to get rid of the family's second home (the old family homestead), a getaway that the couple's children counted on, but he also would have had to dispose of more than half the couple's savings— money he counted on for his own living expenses.

Christine and her husband, Max, who was in a nursing home, owned their $300,000 home, and had been able to put away only $80,000 in savings. For them the spend-down rules meant that the couple could keep the home, but Christine could have only $40,000 in assets, and Max $2,000. The other $38,000 in savings would have to be spent down along with Max's 401(k) that Christine had hoped to live on after Max became ill and required full-time care.

To Qualify for Medicaid

Qualifying for Medicaid is a multistep process that includes:

- *Financial Resource Assessment: The government determines your assets and income (that includes the assets of both husband and wife, if married, and the income of only the institutionalized spouse).*

- *Excluding noncountable assets such as one car, a house (equity under $500,000*; applies to singles or widows only), and certain personal property.*

- *If married, dividing remaining assets in half and determining which assets may be kept under the Spousal Impoverishment Act.*

- *If married, figuring the income of the institutional-ized spouse to determine if it exceeds the allowed amount.*

- *If income and assets of Medicaid applicant exceed the allowed amount, spend-down occurs, unless that person lives in one of a number of states that set*

> *income caps to qualify for Medicaid, and also has a qualified income trust, an irrevocable trust that, when written properly, effectively can remove income from an institutionalized spouse.*
>
> • *If spend-down occurs within the mandated look-back period, penalties are incurred. The penalties are in the form of delayed eligibility for Medicaid based on the amount of spend-down within the violation period, and vary by state.*
>
> **(Some states allow up to $750,000 in equity)*

It's not over yet either. The state government then follows the "name on the check" rule. That is, it looks for where your income comes from and who's getting it. Because Max was the spouse who had worked and therefore received the couple's pension income, and was also the Medicaid applicant, he would be eligible for no more than $1,869 a month (2007; varies by state; adjusted annually for inflation). Any more income than that and he wouldn't qualify for Medicaid to pick up his nursing home costs. (Don't forget to include Social Security, pensions, IRS distribution, investment income, stocks and bonds' dividends/income, and more in the income equation. Even what you pay for Medicare premiums and church tithings count as income for purposes of Medicaid eligibility!)

Fortunately, though, with the right kind of additional financial planning, Medicaid still may cover nursing-home costs for Max and others similar to him whose monthly income is too high for them to qualify for Medicaid, but who still can't afford to foot the entire bill for their care. That's accomplished by establishing what's known as a Miller trust. Max sets up and funds this Miller trust (named after the court case that allowed them), which is actually an irrevocable qualified income trust. He places all his monthly income into the trust, which in turn limits the amount that can be paid out. Those payouts can include insurance premiums, spousal support, and the monthly allowance permitted for the personal needs of Max—the beneficiary. The money left monthly in that trust is paid to the nursing home. Medicaid then pays the remainder of the monthly balance due.

Another alternative: The money in Max's 401(k) and the remaining $38,000 in assets could have been converted into an income stream in the name of Max's wife via a fixed immediate-payout annuity. That's because non-institutionalized spouses such as Max's wife, Christine, can have unlimited monthly income that will not interfere with a spouse's qualifications for Medicaid. At the time of application, Medicaid looks at the couple's assets as a whole, but at the income of the institutionalized spouse only. That's how Andrew, whom we talked about earlier, still was able to have a solid income while his institutionalized wife maintained her Medicaid eligibility.

Beyond the Grave

Uncle Sam and his state government buddies aren't finished with you after death either. The Omnibus Budget Reconciliation Act of 1993 includes a provision called Estate Recovery of Assets for those who were eligible for Medicaid. It mandates that all states may engage in estate recovery, including placing a lien on your home if you qualified for and received Medicaid benefits while alive.

Federal law allows your state to place a lien on your home after your death to recover money paid out by Medicaid for you or your spouse's care.

When applying for Medicaid, the home is a non-countable asset, but if you or your spouse has used Medicaid benefits, the state can place a lien on the home to recover money paid for the nursing-home care. It's not mandatory, but this kind of estate recovery is allowable after the death of both spouses. The state catches these kinds of situations in probate court, so if you set up a revocable living trust, your assets won't go through probate, and thereby, this kind of estate recovery may be avoided.

Your Options to Spend-Down

Now that we've depressed you with reality and discouraged you from counting on Medicaid, let's look at the options you do have.

Residence break. Medicaid allows you to liquidate excess assets and use the cash on your personal residence. Some ways to do so include paying off the mortgage, fixing up the house (new siding, new driveway, new addition), and more. You also can buy a newer, bigger, and more expensive house, or a smaller, more expensive house, as long as you sell your current residence and actually move into the new home.

If you're single, you're also still allowed to keep one car and your residence.

Assets transfer. Another option is to transfer assets to a family member. If you take this tack, however, don't forget the five-year look-back period; otherwise, as a penalty, you or your spouse could be disqualified from receiving Medicaid for a certain length of time. If the transfer was five years ago or longer, you're in the clear. Andrew avoided any Medicaid penalties because he hadn't yet transferred any assets to the couple's kids.

If assets were given to a minor, or someone with a disability who may require long-term care, the best approach is to place the assets in an irrevocable trust. Remember we talked about that in Chapter 2? The trust is the legal entity that holds assets for the benefit of someone else. If it's irrevocable, it's a separate legal entity that cannot be changed once it goes into effect, and its assets are removed from its grantor's assets. If it's revocable, those assets remain part of the grantor's assets and are still under his or her control.

Use those transferred assets. If you've already given your assets to someone else, and the transfer is within the look-back period, consider asking the recipient of the transfer to pick up the tab for your nursing-home care until you're eligible for Medicaid. For example, Randi gave her son most of her assets. Two years later she needed nursing-home care, so her son paid the cost of her care for three years until she met the Medicaid eligibility rules, and Medicaid picked up the tab.

Place assets in a trust. A trust can be an asset-protection device *if* the trust is irrevocable and *if* the asset transfer occurred more than five years ago. That's because placing assets in a trust automatically triggers a five-year look-back. If the transfer occurred within that time period, its value can disqualify someone from Medicaid eligibility for a certain period of time. That's the penalty phase, and is one month for every "x" dollar amount (the amount varies by state). It's generally figured by taking the dollar amount given away and dividing it by the average cost of monthly care in that state. The result is the number of months the individual is ineligible for Medicaid. For example, let's say Mom and Dad gave their children $100,000. Let's assume that the average cost of care in their state is $4,000 a month. That $100,000 that was given away is divided by the $4,000, which equals 25. That means Mom and Dad are ineligible for Medicaid to pick up the cost of their care for 25 months.

Many people mistakenly think that placing assets in a revocable living trust will protect those assets from Medicaid spend-down. That's wrong, and people will pay dearly for that misconception. If you don't have long-term-care insurance, you'll have to liquidate the trust to pay nursing-home costs.

Buy the car of your dreams. If your assets exceed those allowed for Medicaid eligibility, consider buying that pricey—and we seriously mean expensive—car of your dreams. That's because, as we've talked about, Medicaid allows one car to be exempt from spend-down. In many states, it doesn't stipulate what kind of car. So opt for that Rolls Royce, Porsche, or Escalade, and pay cash for it.

A note of caution with this approach: Make sure your state doesn't have limits on the value of that one car.

Annuities. As we've already discussed at length, a properly structured fixed annuity is an excellent way to change an asset to income. If that income is payable to a non-institutionalized spouse, the spouse in a nursing home then still qualifies for Medicaid. Again, all it takes is planning.

Roadmap to Success

Retirees who are veterans, and their spouses, may be eligible for a regular income stream of financial reimbursement for out-of-pocket medical and care expenses if they qualify. You don't have to be a career soldier to qualify, and the benefits definitely are not a handout. They represent a privilege you've earned for your service to our country!

If you don't qualify for the VA benefits, and you've exhausted all other options, you can qualify for Medicaid. Some things to keep in mind when it comes to qualifying for Medicaid:

- Even if you file for Medicaid, chances are you may face hefty out-of-pocket expenses for long-term care for one to two months before Medicaid begins to pick up the tab.
- If you're faced with the prospect of having to spend down assets to qualify for Medicaid, options are available to lessen the financial constraints for

your spouse. They include asset transfers and setting up certain types of trusts.

- Buying a lump-sum annuity can turn an asset into an income stream, and may then, under current laws, enable someone to meet Medicaid qualifications.

- Pay attention to Medicaid's strict look-back rules, which enable the government to examine your finances for the past five years to make sure you haven't given away assets solely to qualify for Medicaid.

- Work with a qualified financial planning expert to make sure that you plan properly for your long-term care needs.

More Resources

- BenefitsCheckUp® (*www.benefitscheckup .org*): The nonprofit National Council on Aging provides this free online service to help anyone find out those private, public, federal, state, and local benefits that they may be entitled to receive.

- Centers for Medicare and Medicaid Services (*www.cms.gov*): The government's official site for Medicaid/Medicare information; click on "Medicaid" for all kinds of valuable information, and applications.

- Covenant Consumer Resource Center (*www .covenantresource.com*): A consumer-oriented Website from Matt Rettick dedicated to helping pre-retirees and retirees access the necessary information to safeguard their estates and become financially fit for life; check out the free booklets available on a variety of topics.

- U.S. Department of Veterans Affairs (*www.va.gov*): The government's official site for information for veterans; click on "Benefits" to access more information on how the VA can help you with care planning.

Epilogue

As you can see, you have a wealth of options in how you approach retirement. Now that we've laid the groundwork for how you can get physically and financially fit, the next step is up to you.

Don't panic. As we've shown you in the past chapters, financial and physical fitness isn't a frightful proposition or a particularly tough one. You simply need to take it seriously and move ahead one step at a time. Whether you're in terrible shape and your body and your finances need a complete overhaul, or you're slightly off in terms of health and wealth and need a little tweaking, we're here to help. We've given you the tools, but you must make the commitment to get started.

The choice is yours. You can toss this book aside, forget all you've read, not change a single thing in your life, and possibly increase your chances of dying younger, dying broke, and suffering chronic and debilitating illnesses along the way. Or you can act now to get physically and financially fit.

As we've emphasized, you don't need to do it all at once. Start with a few easy stretches. Ditch that high-octane soda pop or beer and bag of chips in favor of a healthy fresh-fruit smoothie. Pick up the phone or click on our Website to get the financial help and direction you need to take the next step to prepare fiscally for the future.

If, despite the facts, figures, and warnings, you're still not sure about getting started, look around you at your peers who are physically fit. Do they seem to have more energy? More vitality? Fewer aches and pains and trips to the doctor? Do they radiate a confidence and well-being you wish you had? That goal is within your reach! And what about those friends or acquaintances who don't seem to worry about their financial future? Perhaps you previously considered that kind of fiscal fitness an unachievable dream. It's not, and we hope we have shown you why not.

If you have simply resigned yourself to letting Medicaid take care of you when you're old and infirm, you need to reconsider your strategy. Remember, Medicaid may not pick up that tab. It foots the bill for less than half of those faced with nursing-home care. What will you do if you're not among those who manage to qualify? Who will take care of you? And what if you don't need or want to spend any of your retirement years in a nursing home? Your options are few and far between if you don't plan ahead. Fortunately, it's never too late.

We've given you the roadmap to physical and fiscal fitness in your golden years. Whether you choose to follow that map is up to you. We hope you do. Those who have made the commitment are enjoying their lives to the fullest without needless worrying about the future. You can too!

We also would love to hear from you. Tell us how you're doing on your personal road to physical and fiscal fitness. Send your comments to **info@mattandjack.com**.

Good luck, and enjoy your new lease on life!

Additional Resources

Advantage Compendium list of Top Producers: "Advantage Index Sales and Market Report," 2006: Annuityspecs.com. "2006 Top Ten Producers of Fixed Indexed Annuities (By Sales)."

AHIP (America's Health Insurance Plan): AHIP's Long-Term-Care Policy Checklist.

Alliance for Aging Research: "Long-Term Care over an Uncertain Future: What Can Current Retirees Expect?" *Inquiry* 42: 335–350 (Winter, 2005/2006), Excellus Health Plan, Inc. Authors: Peter Kemper, Harriet Komisar, and Lisa Alexcih.

Employee Benefit Research Institute: "The Retirement System in Transition: The 2007 Retirement Confidence Survey." Authors: Ruth Helman, Mathew Greenwald & Associates; Jack VanDerhei, Temple University and EBRI fellow; and Craig Copeland, EBRI.

Henry J. Kaiser Foundation: "The Distribution of Assets in the Elderly Population Living in the Community," June 2005. "The Uninsured: A Primer—Key Facts about Americans Without Health Insurance," #7451, January 2006. "Medicaid and Long-Term Care," #7089, May 2004. "Deficit Reduction Act of 2005: Implications for Medicaid," #7465, February 2006. "The Distribution of Assets in the Elderly Population Living in the Community," #7335, June 2005.

LTC Consultants: "Long-Term Care: Your Financial Planning Guide," 2007. Author: Phyllis Shelton.

MetLife, Inc.: The MetLife Market Survey of Nursing Home and Home Care Costs, September 2005.

National Council on Aging: "Use Your Home to Stay at Home: Expanding the Use of Reverse Mortgages to Pay for Long-Term Care."

National Mental Health Association: "Signs of Depression."

Pew Research Center: "Baby Boomers: From the Age of Aquarius to the Age of Responsibility," December 2005.

Wharton Financial Institutions Center, Wharton School of Business, University of Pennsylvania: "The Benefits of a Secondary Market for Life Insurance." Authors: Neil A. Doherty and Hal J. Singer.

Glossary

Accelerated death benefit. The ability to tap a portion of a life insurance policy as a living benefit in the event of chronic or terminal disease.

Activities of daily living (ADLs). Basic, everyday personal tasks such as personal hygiene (bathing), mobility (transferring), bathroom duties (toileting and continence), dressing, and eating; the ability to perform any or all of these tasks serves as guideline to determine an individual's outside care needs.

Adult day care. Daily care for adults, most often seniors; can include structured activities, meals, and transportation; can be private or community-based.

Alzheimer's disease. Progressive, irreversible disease with no known cure; a type of dementia that gradually and then profoundly affects one's ability to learn, function, and remember; affects an individual's personality as well.

Annuitant. The individual who purchases/holds an annuity.

Annuity. A contract, most often with an insurance company, that calls for a lump-sum investment or investments throughout time for a specific period.

Asset allocation. An approach to investing that calls for putting a set amount or percentage of your assets—from cash to IRAs to 401(k)s—into different types of investments with different levels of risk and return.

Assisted living. Accommodations, most often for seniors, that provide help with activities of daily living, and include congregate dining, activities, and, in some cases, limited healthcare services, usually at additional charge; can be individual apartments or individual rooms.

Calorie. A measure of an amount of energy stored in a food that the body uses to convert that food to energy; one pound of excess weight equals about 3,500 calories.

Capital gains. Profits from the sale of securities and other investments.

Carbohydrates. The body's main energy source.

Certificate of deposit (CD). Low-risk, FDIC-insured, interest-bearing debt instrument available from banks, credit unions, and savings and loans.

Cholesterol. Substance found in animals and animal products including milk; of two types: HDL, or "good cholesterol"; and LDL, or "bad cholesterol." The latter can build up in the arteries and create problems

Daily guaranteed benefit. That amount of money guaranteed to be paid by an insurer every day for an individual's care in the event that he or she requires short- or long-term care.

Dementia. Progressive loss of mental functions.

Depression. A clinical illness that can be treated once it's identified; not a result of what someone does or eats; neither is it the same as moods, which can be affected by diet.

Do Not Resuscitate order (DNR). A formal, legal directive that stipulates an individual does not want to be revived in the event of a catastrophic medical event such as lung or heart failure.

Dynastride (SM). A dynamic form of walking that involves broad strides while swinging the arms back and forth to their maximum extension; created by health and fitness guru Jack LaLanne.

Elder law. That part of the legal system that involves issues of importance for the aging and elderly.

Elimination period. In relation to long-term care insurance, the time period that must elapse before benefits can be accessed; the deduction period.

Equity. An ownership interest in any property. It is often used to refer to ownership in a company, and is evidenced by ownership of shares of various types of stock.

Exchange traded funds (ETFs). Also known as an index fund, made up of stocks in a specific index such as the Standard and Poor's 500 or Dow Jones Industrial Average; not actively managed, so lower cost than a mutual fund; not considered a mutual fund because of certain trading specifications and limitations.

Fiber. Substance found in certain foods, especially whole grains, that's part of good nutrition; often referred to as "bulk"; eat it regularly to help with elimination.

Fixed indexed annuity. Formerly known as an equity indexed annuity; a fixed annuity that pegs its earnings on a major market index such as the S&P 500, Dow Jones Industrial Average.

Funeral directive. A formal document (not legal and binding) that lays out an individual's wishes with regard to the details of any ceremonies and burial, as well as how the body will be handled after death.

Grantor. The individual who establishes and funds a trust.

Immediate annuity. A contract—annuity—most often with an insurance company, that calls for a lump-sum investment or investments throughout time for a specific period with payout beginning as soon as it's funded.

Inflation protection. For purposes of long-term-care insurance, automatic daily benefit increase to protect policyholder from future increases in cost of care due to rising prices throughout time.

In-home care. Assistance provided to an individual, often elderly, at his or her place of residence, as opposed to that person having to move to an assisted-living facility or nursing home.

Intestate. When an individual dies without a will.

IRA, multigenerational. Also a stretch IRA, an individual retirement account that, at its owner's death, has no lump-sum income taxes due on earnings; the vast majority of the balance instead continues to grow because only small minimum annual withdrawals are required and thus potentially subject to taxation; also available as an annuity.

Legal guardianship. A formal legal document, or clause as part of a last will and testament, that stipulates who will care for any dependents, and how.

Life insurance. A legal contract/policy whereby, in exchange for pay-in of a certain amount of money, usually in the form of regular premiums, a sum of money will be paid out to a specified beneficiary/beneficiaries at policyholder's death.

Life settlement. An option for the chronically or terminally ill; involves selling an unwanted or unnecessary life insurance policy back to the insurer or to a third party for more than its surrender value and less than its net death benefit (the amount paid out at death, less any debts due on the policy).

Living will. A legal document that stipulates an individual's wishes with regard to various types of artificial life support or nutrition in the event of a catastrophic medical event.

Long-term care. Also known as LTC, the need by many Americans of all ages for prolonged medical and/or physical assistance in a variety of settings; a contract involving long-term care should stipulate the types of long-term care covered or required.

Long-term-care insurance. A type of indemnity coverage that helps an individual defray the high cost of long-term care in a variety of settings in exchange for regular premiums paid; any contract involving long-term-care insurance should stipulate the types of care and settings covered by policy.

Look-back rule. The legal ability for the government to review a Medicaid applicant's past finances up to a certain number of years to ascertain if the applicant truly qualifies on the basis of financial need and didn't just divest high assets for the purposes of obtaining free care.

Magic Five. Jack LaLanne's series of exercises that represent a great way to start your every day with physical and mental fitness in mind.

Market capitalization. For investment purposes, can provide insight into the risk level of a company; figured by multiplying the number of outstanding shares of the stock by the stock price.

Medicaid. A state-administered, federally funded government program that provides medical care to the poor.

Medicare. A federal medical program available to those age 65 and up that helps alleviate the high cost of medical care with restrictions and limitations; requires co-payments and deductibles.

Medicaid-friendly annuity: An annuity that can be annuitized or converted to an income stream for an at-home spouse; must be irrevocable, unassignable, and paid out within the owner's life span.

Medigap. Private-pay insurance, with restrictions, qualifications, and limitations, that is designed to pick up medical costs not paid by Medicare.

Mineral. Important substance for general health, growth, and body maintenance; the body doesn't manufacture minerals.

Modified endowment contract (MEC). Basically a life insurance policy that's over-funded up-front so it has a high cash value that in turn can be tapped to pay the costs of long-term care in the event of chronic illness and need.

Monounsaturates. Another "safe" fat; includes olive oil, canola (rape-seed) oil, and peanut oils.

Mutual fund. A company that sells its shares to the public in order to raise money to invest in other types of investments to generate profits for its shareholders.

Net death benefit. With a life insurance policy, the amount paid out at death, less any debts due on the policy.

Obesity. The condition of being extremely fat; grossly over-weight.

Payable on death (POD). A legal stipulation as part of holding an asset that designates a specific individual or organization to receive that asset at the death of the original owner; avoids any delays of probate.

Polyunsaturates. Harmless fats that can have beneficial side effects; oils include safflower oil, soybean oil, corn oil, cottonseed oil, sesame oil, sunflower oils, and most margarines.

Power of attorney (POA). Naming another individual to handle certain of your affairs when you're no longer able to do so yourself.

> **Durable.** Goes into effect as soon as it's signed, and remains in effect should you become incapacitated and until you die or the courts remove the power.

> **Springing.** Set to go into effect at a later time, usually only when you are declared incompetent or some other event occurs as named in the document.

> **Healthcare.** Individual(s) to make healthcare decisions in the event that you're unable to do so yourself; also known as healthcare proxy.

> **Finance.** Individual(s) to take care of your financial matters if you become incapacitated and no longer can do so yourself.

Preexisting condition. Medical condition that already existed or was diagnosed prior to an event; with long-term-care insurance, for example, an illness or issue that existed before applying for a policy.

Principal. Original amount invested.

Probate. Legal process in which a will is determined to be legal and valid.

Protein. Substance fundamental for living cells; normal adults and growing children require 1 gram of protein for every 2.2 pounds (equal to 1 kilogram) of body weight.

Repetitions (reps). The number of times to repeat an exercise.

Reverse mortgage. A specialized loan that enables those age 62 and older to tap the equity in their homes to generate income and still live in their homes.

Saturates. Troublesome fats that include coconut oil, palm kernel and palm oils, and hydrogenated oils; also includes whole milk dairy products, butter, lard, and other animal products.

Section 529 plan. Usually referred to as simply a *529 plan*, this is a tax-advantaged savings vehicle for higher education expenses; earnings inside an account grow tax-free; distributions are tax-free if used for a qualified higher-education expense

Set. With regard to exercising, a specific number of times to repeat a specific exercise.

Small cap fund. Jargon for *small capitalization fund*, which is a pool of stocks in smaller companies—generally those with a market capitalization (number of outstanding shares of the stock multiplied by the stock price) of $500 million or less.

Spend-down. With regard to Medicaid, the necessity of an individual to divest his or her assets in order to qualify for it.

Starch. A complex carbohydrate that's found in foods such as potatoes, wheat, corn, and rice.

Trust. A legal entity that holds its assets for the purposes of someone or something else; assets held in a trust avoid delays of probate.

> **Irrevocable.** A trust that's a separate legal entity; directed by a trustee; files its own tax return.
>
> **Revocable.** A trust that remains under its grantor's control and direction; it remains part of the grantor's assets for purposes of taxes; trust assets avoid probate delays at death of grantor.
>
> **Living.** A trust established by an individual while he or she is alive.
>
> **Testamentary.** A trust set up by a will that goes into effect at a person's death.

Viatical settlement. A form of life settlement in which a terminally ill person sells his or her life insurance policy in exchange for cash while alive.

Vitamins. Essential nutrients for the body; can be either fat- or water-soluble

Will. A formal legal document that stipulates an individual's desires with regard to disbursement of his or her property and assets after death; can include a *legal guardianship* clause that stipulates who will care for any dependents, and how.

Index

About the Authors

Jack LaLanne is recognizable to three generations as *the* Godfather of Fitness. Jack has devoted seven decades to coaching others on television and in person about what it takes to get healthy, stay healthy and live a fulfilling life. As host of the longest-running television fitness show—*The Jack LaLanne Show*—Jack used this medium to create public awareness for the need for systematic physical conditioning through rigorous daily exercise and diet.

Jack is constantly stunning his audience with shocking physical feats, such as swimming from Alcatraz with hands and feet shackled, breaking physical barriers to prove that anything can be done if you put your mind to it. At the age of 93, Jack is *the* prime example that if you follow his advice, you will look and feel great!

Jack currently resides in Morro Bay, California, with Elaine, his wife of 53 years.

Matthew J. Rettick knows what it takes to plan for a great retirement. Founder and CEO of Covenant Reliance Producers, LLC, Rettick is a respected retirement and estate planner, who has spent decades teaching retirees and preretirees nationwide how to become fiscally fit *and* stay that way. An in-demand national speaker, Matthew is tapped for financial product advice from insurance companies as well as various television stations for his expert advice. Recognized by industry experts as "the man with the plan," Matthew has made a personal commitment to help ensure that a person's assets *last*. His contribution to *Fiscal Fitness* gives readers of all ages a plan to follow to achieve the best possible financial future.

Matthew and his wife, Linda, live north of Nashville, Tennessee. They have four children and 13 grandchildren.

Matt and Jack Have Additional Information to Help You on Your Way to Physical and Financial Fitness!!

Check the Box for Each Topic You Want
to Learn More About!

Your FREE Financial Tools:

- ❑ *Growth Without Risk* — The Safe and Secure Way to Earn Stock Market-Linked Returns Without Market Risk to Your Principal

- ❑ *Legal Issues* — Important Documents You Need to Put in Place **NOW!**

- ❑ *Medicaid Spend-Down* — Don't Let Your Assets Disappear if You Need Nursing Home Care!

- ❑ *IRA's/401(k)* — 8 Signs Your IRA/401(k) is Broken, and How to Fix It!

- ❑ *Reverse Mortgages* — The Good, the Bad, and the Benefits

- ❑ *Professional Money Management* — Earn Better Returns While Reducing Taxes and Fees

- ❑ *Estate Planning* — Make Sure Your Money Ends up in the Right Hands!

- ❑ *Long-Term Care Insurance* — Why You Need It, and How to Afford It!!

TO OBTAIN YOUR FREE COPIES, SIMPLY TEAR OUT AND FAX TO **615-620-1340**, CALL **800-816-3857**, or visit *www.covenantresource.com* TODAY!

Your Fitness Tools:

For more information on Jack LaLanne's products and his lifestyle, please visit *www.jacklalanne.com*!